Karl Marx

D1263972

Karl Marx

Founder of Modern Communism

by
ARNOLD KETTLE

ROY PUBLISHERS, INC.
New York

MADE AND PRINTED IN GREAT BRITAIN BY
MORRISON AND GIBB LIMITED, LONDON AND EDINBURGH

Library of Congress Catalog Card Number 64–10671

For Martin and Nicholas

CONTENTS

LIST OF ILLUSTRATIONS

The author acknowledges the help of Mr Frank Jackson in obtaining illustrations 3, 4, 5, 6, 7, 9, and 10, which are reproduced by permission of the Communist Party of Great Britain. Illustrations 1, 2, 8, and the jacket photograph are reproduced by permission of the Marx Memorial Library, and the author acknowledges the help of Mr Andrew Rothstein in obtaining them.

INTRODUCTION

To THE north of London, as every Londoner knows, lie the twin hills of Hampstead and Highgate. From the southern slopes of the hills on a clear day you get a fine view of the city, spreading out in its beauty and ugliness from both banks of the Thames. It was on Highgate hill that Dick Whittington heard the bells ringing which drew him back to London, and it was nearby that David Copperfield went to stay at Steerforth's home and, later, found the cottage where he lived with Dora.

In 1849, the year *David Copperfield* was being published as a serial, Karl Marx, a German refugee, came to settle in London. For most of the next thirty-four years, Marx lived within easy reach of the twin hills and, more than in any other part of London, he delighted in Hampstead Heath where, week in week out, he walked and picnicked and spent his summer Sundays with his family. When he died, he was buried in Highgate Cemetery, just below what is now Waterlow Park.

Today, Marx's grave is the most striking in the Cemetery. It is marked by a large, immensely solid-looking block of stone, surmounted by a huge impressive head. The head is somewhat out of proportion to the stone which carries it, giving a rather squat effect; yet the monument has a strange appropriateness about it, a suggestion of power still unfulfilled, close to the earth yet dominating it. When Marx was buried, on March 17, 1883, his friend Frederick Engels made the farewell speech at his graveside. The first sentence he spoke was:

'On the afternoon of the fourteenth of March at a quarter to three the greatest living thinker ceased to think'.

It is doubtful whether a thousand people could have been found in London in 1883 to whom Engels's words would not have seemed the wildest of exaggerations. During the following twenty years or so it is certain that visitors to Highgate Cemetery were more likely to wish to pay their tribute to George Eliot or G. H. Lewes or Herbert Spencer, all of whom are buried within a few yards of his grave, than to Karl Marx. Yet if you visit the place today these other graves are only very seldom remembered, while at the foot of Marx's monument there are always flowers. If you stop to read the cards attached to the wreaths and bunches of flowers that lie there you will almost certainly find that they come from visitors from all over the world—'From a group of Soviet Tourists', 'From an Indian comrade', 'From the Central Committee of the Communist Party of China', 'From some visitors from Venezuela', 'From the London District Committee of the Communist Party on May Day', 'From Major Yuri Gagarin'.

On the gravestone, besides the names of Karl Marx and his family who lie buried there, are inscribed two sentences, perhaps the most famous their author wrote. One reads: 'The philosophers have only interpreted the world in various ways; the point, however, is to change it'. The second: 'Workers of all lands, unite'.

PART ONE

MARX'S LIFE

WHEN KARL MARX came to London in 1849 he was thirty-one years old. He brought with him his wife and three small children and a family servant named Lenchen Demuth who, as time went on, became more and more a part of the family, a loved and trusted friend. Shortly after they had settled in London, Frau Marx had another baby. For a time they lived in Chelsea, but later moved into a house in Dean Street, Soho, where they lived in two rooms.

The Marxes were refugees, and the life they lived in London was not unlike the sort of life which, in the nineteen-thirties, thousands more German refugees in London, fleeing from Hitler's Germany, led. They were middle-class people, the kind of people who in those days as a matter of course would be provided by their parents with a servant; though few middle-class couples with a growing family had the luck to have a servant like Lenchen, who was so devoted to the family that she stuck to them through all their difficulties and shared their joys and hopes.

The Marxes came from Trier, an historic German city near the French border. Karl Marx had been born in 1818, the son of a prosperous lawyer. The girl he married, Jenny von Westphalen, had been a childhood friend.

The Westphalens lived near the Marxes; they, too, were well-to-do, connected with the minor aristocracy. Karl had been sent as a matter of course to the university and, like a German student to this day, shifted from one university to another in the course of his studies—Bonn, Berlin, Jena—beginning as a student of Law, but quickly finding that his main interests lay in history and philosophy.

Marx's family, then, was comfortably off and cultured. It was, on both sides, a Jewish family, but Marx's father gave up the Jewish religion and Karl himself does not seem to have ever had any religious beliefs. It was a happy family, and Marx had also a very warm affection for Jenny's father; his 'dear fatherly friend' he called him.

How did it come about that such people should settle as refugees in a cramped house in Soho in 1849, and remain in exile till Karl and Jenny Marx died and were buried in Highgate Cemetery?

To understand the story fully, it is necessary to know a good deal about the history of Europe a hundred years and more ago. Something of that history will emerge in the course of this book, but for the moment we are concerned with the more personal side of the story.

Karl Marx was a refugee because, by 1849, he had become a convinced revolutionary, and there was no freedom for revolutionaries in the Germany of his day. He had had to leave his country first in 1843, when he was twenty-five and recently married. At that time he was working as a journalist and had become editor of

The Rhineland Newspaper published in Cologne. It was an Opposition paper, outspoken in its criticism of the Government, and as a result the Government banned it. Marx was not surprised. 'The atmosphere was becoming too oppressive for me', he wrote to a colleague. 'It is a bad thing to work in servitude and to fight with pinpricks instead of with the sword, even in the cause of freedom. I am tired of the hypocrisy, the stupidity, and the brutality of the authorities, and of our submissiveness. . . . There is nothing more I can do in Germany. One debases oneself here.'

And so, in 1843, Marx, like many of his friends, including Heinrich Heine the poet, had left Germany for Paris, where he believed there would be more freedom to work and write and from where he proposed to edit a new German Review which would carry on the fight for freedom in his own country. This first exile from Germany lasted for five years, the first two spent in Paris, the next three in Brussels. Even when he was away from his homeland, the Prussian authorities did not leave Marx in peace but managed to persuade the French Government to expel him from France, which was why he moved to Brussels, where he continued to work and write articles and his first books. The books are concerned with philosophy, but this did not mean that Marx was becoming more academic, less interested in politics and public affairs. On the contrary, it was in this first period of exile, between 1843 and 1848, that Karl Marx reached the conclusions that led him to collaborate with Frederick Engels in writing *The*

Communist Manifesto. It was in Brussels that he became a communist.

In 1848, the year in which revolutions took place in so many countries on the continent of Europe, the Marxes were able to return home to Germany, and once more Marx started a newspaper. But the *New Rhineland Newspaper* had as difficult a career as its predecessor. This time the first problem was a financial one, for as Marx's views became more left-wing and less respectable it became harder to persuade rich people to finance the paper. But the more fundamental problem was the failure of the 1848 revolution. Instead of bringing into being a truly democratic society in which the workers had full freedom, the revolution had merely, Marx believed, resulted in increased power for the prosperous middle class, the business-men and bankers and industrialists. This was not what he and Engels were interested in. And so, once it again proved impossible to find in Germany the freedom to work and publish, the Marx family, now growing in size, went into exile, this time never to return to their homeland for more than short visits.

The life of a refugee is seldom, in the nature of things, a happy one, and the first years the Marxes spent in London were anything but easy. There was very little money, and it was often hard to scrape together enough to pay the rent. Marx eventually got a regular job as European correspondent of the *New York Tribune*, but this brought in little enough. Visits to the 'pop shop', under the sign of the three brass balls, were frequent.

Two of the four elder children died, and then a fifth baby, born in 1850, died also before she was two. Jenny Marx's letters tell their own story of hardship and misery.

'At Easter 1852 our poor little Franzeska fell ill with severe bronchitis. For three days the poor child struggled against death and suffered much. Her small lifeless body rested in our little back room whilst we all went together into the front room and when night came we made up beds on the floor. The three surviving children lay with us and we cried for the poor little angel who now rested so cold and lifeless in the next room. The poor child's death took place in a period of bitterest poverty. I went to a French fugitive who lives near us and who had visited us shortly before. He received me with friendliness and sympathy and gave me two pounds, and with that money the coffin in which my child could rest peacefully was paid for. It had no cradle when it was born and even the last little shell was denied it long enough.'

How could cultured, scholarly people, brought up in generous comfort, put up with such a life in a foreign land, surrounded by other 'displaced persons', refugees involved in the most bitter and frustrating quarrels and arguments? What sustained Karl Marx, and led him to accept such a life almost as a matter of course, was his complete confidence in the truth of his ideas and the justice of the cause he served. What sustained Jenny Marx and the children was their complete confidence in this man whom official society—the 'Establishment' of the day—regarded as a dangerous fanatic.

What kind of a man was he? A stocky, powerfully built man, with a magnificent head, a thick black beard, and sharp, penetrating dark eyes. Among the refugees he was often known as 'Papa Marx' or 'The Old Man', though in fact he was still quite young, because his wisdom and the solid weight of experience and character behind him made him seem a natural leader and older than his years. His children, who adored him, christened him 'The Moor' because he was so dark.

He was a tremendous worker. Soon after his arrival in London he decided that, for the time being, he would withdraw from the political arguments of the refugees, which he found demoralizing, and devote himself to study and writing, the production of his great book *Capital* which he believed would do more than anything else to help the revolutionary cause. Month in, month out, he spent the whole day in the library of the British Museum, absorbing works of history, philosophy, and economics, ransacking official publications and government reports, piling up facts. And then at home, far into the night, he would go on working, sustained by black coffee and tobacco. Social life, except on Sundays, he had little of, though he would give his time freely to those who came to consult him and seek his advice on problems of the revolutionary movement.

Marx was a remarkable linguist. He wrote German, French, and English fluently, and had a working knowledge of a dozen other languages. In his late fifties he began to learn Russian. Every year, one of his sons-in-law recorded, he used to read the plays of Aeschylus in the Greek. And he was an enthusiastic reader of more modern literature, loving especially the novels of Balzac and Fielding and the plays of Shakespeare, many of which he knew by heart. Marx was, in fact, a deeply cultured man who delighted in the great human achievements of the past. 'Nothing human is foreign to me', was one of his favourite sayings. He was a revolutionary because he came to believe in the necessity of fundamental social change, not because he had a chip on his shoulder.

Obviously such a man had strong and even passionate convictions and feelings. His eyes would light up with anger and indignation when he spoke of injustice and oppression; but Marx was not one who believed that anger in itself does much good. What he was chiefly interested in was facts—the actual facts of the existing world and how they could be changed; and even in the height of argument his indignation would quickly be followed by a sober detailed stream of information, a dispassionate review of the facts of the situation and what could be done about them.

There was little in his life of what the world of his time would have called success. Many hardships, many disappointments. He cannot always have been an easy man to live with; so absorbed would he become in the work on hand that the day-to-day business of household chores, social visits, coming to meals on time, would often get ignored, and sometimes when he was in a bad mood it took Lenchen, with her blunt country commonsense, to bring him back to the world of family facts and necessities. But though Marx had his share of depression and disappointment and illness, the devotion of his family and friends is the best proof of his humanity. He was particularly good with children. 'It's children who ought to educate their parents', he used to say; and however busy and absorbed he was, he was not too busy to spend time and energy with his daughters.

One of his friends, Karl Liebknecht, has described vividly a Sunday outing with the Marx family in the easier period after their first time of desperate poverty in London. The favourite outing was to Hampstead Heath, a good hour and a half's walk from the Soho home. Other refugees would join the family on a Sunday morning and the children would lead the way, with some of their friends. Then Karl and Jenny Marx and one or two of the more staid and perhaps older guests would proceed with more dignity and serious conversation, and the rear would be brought up by Lenchen and some of the younger refugees who had attached themselves to the Marx ménage; they carried the food, preferably a joint of cold roast veal, which would be supplemented by bread and cheese and beer at 'Jack Straw's Castle' or one of the other pubs on the Heath. After lunch the Marx 'camp' would turn to various pastimes, games, races, and, above all, donkey-rides. And then, as the party wended its way home downhill, they would sing, as any group of Germans on such occasions always will, the familiar sentimental folk songs of their homeland.

Even the degree of comfort and relaxation which such

expeditions reveal would not have been possible without the help of the man who, more than any other, shared Karl Marx's life and aspirations. Frederick Engels, like Marx, came of a well-to-do German family. His father was a partner in the big spinning firm of Ermen and Engels in Manchester. In many respects, Engels was the opposite of Marx: tall, fair-haired, quick and fluent and witty, with a great deal of social charm and ease, mingling easily with the 'gentry' among whom he lived. But he was the equal of Marx in devotion to the communist cause which as a young man, an army officer, he had come to associate himself with.

Engels was a brilliant man, extraordinarily well-informed on an almost incredible range of subjects from military strategy to the natural sciences. He had wanted to give up his job in his father's business to devote himself entirely to the working-class movement; but he came to the conclusion that, in this difficult time when socialists and revolutionaries were being driven from country to country and had often the greatest difficulty in getting a job, it was essential that he, who had the opportunity to keep up a regular income, should do so and thereby help his comrades and cause. So he remained in the family business in Manchester, a familiar and popular figure among the local business-men there, at the same time as he gave his heart and soul and money to the people who were bent on taking power from these very business-men.

The friendship of Marx and Engels was a remarkable one, so long and close and rewarding. They were in their twenties when they first met; and from that time on, especially after the Marxes' arrival in England in 1849, until Karl's death in 1883, it was rare for a week to pass without a meeting or a letter. Karl Marx had an unreserved respect for Engels's judgment, unfailing confidence in his personal and intellectual powers; they were, in the fullest possible sense, collaborators and sharers. Engels was, of all the visitors at Marx's home, the most welcome: and it was to Engels's home that, after the deaths of Jenny and Karl Marx, Lenchen Demuth went to live. Financially, it was Engels's help that kept the Marx family going.

Marx and Engels were both prodigious workers and wrote a great deal. After the early works, *The Communist Manifesto* and *The German Ideology*, on which they collaborated, it might be said that Marx tended to concentrate on economics and history, Engels on philosophy and natural science. But to put it this way is somewhat misleading. For one thing, all their work involved to some extent collaboration, and neither was interested in the personal credit of claiming 'I did it'. For another, it was part of the outlook that Marx and Engels developed, to emphasize that life and the world and mankind's thoughts cannot be divided into water-tight compartments. *All* systematized knowledge which stood the test of time and experience, Marx regarded as science. History and political economy, though they could not be measured with the same sort of instruments or accuracy as those used in physics or even biology, were themselves sciences. The truest philosophy was the one that turned out to be the most scientific—that is to say, to fit and explain the facts of reality and therefore to formulate laws about the way it works. So Marx's books, *Capital*, *The Critique of Political Economy*, *The Civil War in France*, and Engels's *Anti-Dühring* and *Dialectics of Nature* cannot really be put into pigeon-holes marked Economics, Politics, History, Science, etc. They are all about aspects of the world and the way it works, and not one aspect can be wholly separated from the others. Some of the most potent *philosophical* remarks of Marx occur in books apparently dealing with economic matters; Engels's *Anti-Dühring*, a book based on a number of philosophical arguments with a now otherwise forgotten German thinker named Dühring, contains the fullest short account of Marxist *political* thinking, the section on socialism, what it involves and how ideas about it have changed.

It was not, however, simply in writing books and articles that Karl Marx spent the thirty-four years he lived in London. His researches and writing—'scientific work' he always called it—occupied the major part of his time and, for months on end, sometimes entirely dominated it; but even the publication of *Capital* was not seen by Marx as an end in itself. It was merely one contribution to the struggle to change the world. And changing the world was a matter, Marx insisted, of actions, not simply preaching. Books helped men to change the world but did not do the job for them.

The main thing, therefore, was to use the books. There would be no point in books about electricity if we did not use electricity. Electricity is not just a 'subject' for study; it is a power. And the same, Marx held, is true

23

of all important subjects, philosophy and economics included.

And politics, the practical science of social change, was to Marx not something to be left to professional politicians who go in for it as a career. To be serious about life was to face the need to investigate the world and change it; to be serious about changing the world meant taking political action. If you don't take political action, it doesn't mean that no political action is taken; it merely means that other people take it—that politics is, so to speak, a part of life handed over to other people. To Marx it seemed essential that if the people were to control their own destiny they should take politics seriously; and taking politics seriously meant action and organization.

That is why Karl Marx spent a considerable part of his time helping to organize political activity, especially among the working class. There was at that time no Labour movement of the sort we now know in Britain; even though in Britain, the first highly-industrialized country in Europe, there were already the beginnings of such a movement.

Marx had many friends among the early British socialists and working-class leaders. These included men like Ernest Jones and Julian Harney, who had been among the leaders of the powerful Chartist movement, and also some of those who were beginning to organize Trade Unions. It was at the initiative of Marx, some of the refugees from the Continent, and some of the British Trade Union leaders, that the International Working-Men's Association—the First International as it came to be called—was founded in 1864 at a meeting in the St Martin's Hall, in London.

Delegates came to this meeting from the working-class movements of France, Germany, Switzerland, and Belgium. It was the first gathering of its kind in the world, based on the idea that the workers of the world, no matter what their nationality, have at bottom the same interests. Fifteen years before, *The Communist Manifesto* had called on the workers of all lands to unite; the existence of the International began the long struggle to transform this slogan from a hope into a practical possibility.

Marx played a very active part in the politics of 'the International' and was at all times regarded as its leader and moving spirit. The history of his political struggles and arguments from 1864 until his death is a long and complicated story, involving successes and setbacks, bitter disputes and generous tributes.

The problems of the young working-class movement were bound to be considerable. Conditions in the different countries themselves differed a good deal, and so did the traditional ideas of the left-wing movements which had had diverse histories. Lack of experience inevitably led to all kinds of doubts and disputes about strategy and tactics. What ought to be the attitude of militant socialists to trade unions? Do they help the struggle for social change or hold it back by diverting the workers' attention to purely bread-and-butter problems? Ought working-class political leaders to have anything to do with Parliaments, or will such institutions tend to corrupt them? Is it ever in the interests of the workers to support a war?

What ought to be the attitude of working-class parties to nationalism?

A score of such fundamental questions and a hundred others concerned with immediate tactics faced the growing revolutionary movement. It was inevitable that the answering of them should involve bitter disagreements and many mistakes.

If Marx seems sometimes to have been excessively sharp and intolerant in some of the political disputes in which he became involved, we should remember that in the formative years of any great movement it is always necessary for the leadership to fight uncompromisingly to get certain underlying principles recognized. He was convinced that unless the working-class movement freed itself completely from what he held to be 'bourgeois ideas' (that is to say, the ways of thinking and the unconscious prejudices of the middle class) it would never carry through the socialist revolution which was necessary to humanity. He therefore considered it essential to carry on a continuous campaign in his published writings and private letters against those policies which he believed would prove fatal to the aims of the International and those leaders who would, consciously or unconsciously, betray the cause. Perhaps the most bitter of his arguments were those with and about the German socialist Lassalle and the Russian anarchist Bakunin.

That Marx was in every instance right in his judgments neither he nor his followers would have claimed, for he did not consider himself more than human; but that it was necessary to thrash out quite ruthlessly in argument and through experience the problems involved in building an independent working-class movement—this he never doubted.

The International carried on for about eight years, and during that time it was Marx's most active preoccupation. He visited most of the countries involved in the movement during that period, wrote pamphlets, prepared resolutions, exchanged ideas and gave advice. And he had the satisfaction of seeing in his lifetime another decisive step forward in the communist movement.

In 1871, after the defeat of the French army by the Germans, the workers of Paris drove out the discredited government and established a new state, the Commune, which Marx, as well as the French working-class leaders, held to be the most advanced and democratic state up till then achieved in history. The Paris Commune lasted for ten weeks before it was overthrown by the right-wing. The massacre of the *communards* that followed was appalling. Something like a hundred thousand Parisians were killed or exiled. For socialists the destruction of the Commune was a tragedy. But even in the blackest hour of defeat Marx refused to be demoralized. He wrote: 'The Paris of the workers with its Commune will be commemorated for ever as the glorious herald of a new society. Its martyrs are enshrined in the great heart of the working class.'

The defeat of the Commune meant, for the moment, the end of the International. It also had a by-product which affected Marx's life considerably, for it brought a new wave of refugees to England, among them two

French communards—Paul Lafargue and Charles Longuet, who were to marry his two elder daughters, Laura and Jenny. Marx and his wife were happy in their girls' marriages, and there was a warm affection between Marx and his French sons-in-law.

*   *   *   *   *

The eighteen-seventies was for Marx a period of renewed work on the later volumes of *Capital*, a somewhat easier financial situation, and a good deal of ill-health. The family had moved in 1856 from Dean Street to Grafton Terrace, Haverstock Hill, near Hampstead Heath, and in 1875 they again moved house, this time to Maitland Park Road, not far away.

In the years following the Paris Commune the political situation looked, from Marx's point of view, black enough, but in the late seventies new possibilities seemed to be arising. The French working-class movement was recovering from its defeat, the socialist movement in Germany was growing powerful, and in Britain the growth of the trades unions and socialist ideas, with the emergence of such figures as H. M. Hyndman and William Morris, had begun. *Capital* had been translated into several languages, including Russian, and all over the world groups of revolutionaries were beginning (somewhat to the distaste of Marx himself) to call themselves Marxists.

In 1881 Jenny Marx, after an illness she had borne with extraordinary courage, died of cancer. In his youth Marx had been proud of his wife's beauty; by the end of

(*Above*) Trier, Marx's birthplace, from a contemporary print. (*Below*) The Friedrich-Wilhelm school in Trier, which Marx attended from 1830 to 1835.

Jenny Marx

her life he had come to realize all that he owed to her selfless loyalty and strength of character; she had been far more than 'the great man's wife', a woman of great intelligence who shared her husband's interests and convictions because she understood them. Her death and that of his daughter Jenny Longuet were terrible blows to Marx. Thirty years earlier, young and in good health, he had been able to override personal troubles. But Engels, seeing him the day his wife died, said to his youngest daughter Eleanor: 'Moor has died too'. Eleanor was angry with Engels at the time, thinking it a defeatist thing to say, but she came to see that what he said was true:

'He struggled hard to keep going', she wrote afterwards, 'for he was a fighter to the last—but he was a broken man. . . . For him there was something which stood above everything else—that was his devotion to the cause. He attempted to complete his great work. . . .'

He was, however, very ill, and on March 14, 1883,

'Moor went from his bedroom into the study in Maitland Park, sat in the armchair and tranquilly went to sleep'.

PART TWO

CHAPTER I

MARX AS AN ECONOMIST

ECONOMICS IS the study of the way a society is organized for the production of its material needs and the distribution of what is produced. Production, the creating of the material things which human beings need—food, clothing, houses, means of transport, and so on—is essential to the continuance of human life. If, every day of every year, hundreds of millions of people in all parts of the world did not work, and as a result, produce things, we could not live the sort of lives that human beings have come to think of as human.

Karl Marx did not begin as an economist. It was only as he became interested in the political struggle to change the world that he gradually came to feel the supreme importance of economics. As he grew older he became more and more convinced that without a thorough mastery of the science of economics it was impossible either to understand the truth about the world he lived in or to see how to build a different society. His economic ideas are therefore of particular importance in any consideration of Marx's work. They may be said (we shall come back to this question later) to be *fundamental* to his contribution to human thought; that is why we shall consider them first.

Marx's ideas about economics did not, of course, begin from nothing. He never pretended that he did not learn a lot from other people, and in this connection the thinkers from whom he learned most were the British economists, particularly Adam Smith and David Ricardo. Adam Smith's book *The Wealth of Nations* (published in 1776) had been the first really thorough-going attempt to analyse and explain how the world of the era of modern trade and commerce actually worked. It was not by chance, Marx believed, that the serious study of economics (or political economy as he preferred to call it) began in Britain, for in the 18th and 19th centuries Britain was the most 'advanced' nation commercially, the country in which modern methods of production and trade had been first developed; and naturally the British business-men and bankers above all others needed to understand what they were doing as well as doing it. For though men can often do what they do without understanding all about it, understanding always helps them to do it better. It is only when things are going badly for them, and they sense that the discovery of more of the truth would be unpleasant and perhaps painful for them, that people begin to be afraid of knowledge and science. The British merchants and bankers of Adam Smith's time were not afraid; and as a consequence he and, a little later, Ricardo, were able to tell a great deal of the truth about the workings of their society.

The principal idea of the British economists which

Karl Marx recognized as deeply important was what is called the labour theory of value. The essence of this theory is that all forms of wealth, created for purposes of exchange, get their value from the work put into producing them. Human labour is in this sense the source of human wealth, for everything you have, except what is actually found in nature, someone has worked to produce. All exchange-values are, in fact, the result of the application of human labour to something already there, and found free in nature.

The capacity of men to make wealth out of what nature provides depends, we all know, on his ability to invent and use tools. Primitive man spends all his time working for the barest necessities which will keep him and his family alive—hunting, gathering fruits, protecting himself from other men and animals and the weather. Compared with us he is poor, because, although he works for many hours, he has few tools and his own labour therefore produces very little. Also he is as yet in no position to co-operate fruitfully with other men so that their joint labour may improve things. In modern, complicated societies, the relation between a person's wealth and the labour that goes to produce it is not so obvious. Indeed, as Marx pointed out, many of the people who have the greatest wealth do not do much work at all. How can they, therefore, have wealth? Because, as we all know, they have money. But money, though it is a *symbol* of wealth (i.e. represents such-and-such an amount of wealth) is not a *source* of wealth. Robinson Crusoe quickly discovered this: money on his island was worth nothing to him, his skill with his hands and brain worth everything. Money is, in fact, a symbol of wealth just so long as other people are prepared to recognize it as such. And they are in fact prepared to do this as long as they recognize that it stands for an actual amount of labour. Crusoe's money was of no use to him because there was no one on his island with whom he could exchange it for other products of labour.

Marx held that an understanding of the labour theory of value was essential to any firm grasp of the economics of existing society. The chief reason he emphasized this was because, as we shall see in a moment, he noted that the whole system he was describing involved the exchange of commodities. Everything depended on exchange, on buying and selling; and therefore it was essential to discover the basis for such exchange, the value of the various commodities. Marx did not suggest, of course, that the labour theory of value explained every detail of the way an economy works. He did not look on it as a simple infallible way of discovering the prices of things from day to day. What was important was to realize that, despite the complexity of modern economic organization, human labour remained the only ultimate source of exchange value. Many factors affect the particular prices at which at particular times particular goods are exchanged, but nothing alters the basic fact that without work no value can be produced.

Marx emphasized this point all the more strongly because in modern societies it tends to be veiled, hidden from the grasp of the man in the street. And Marx believed there was a reason for this too. He came to the conclusion that it suited the book of the rich to try to conceal the fact that labour is the source of wealth; for immediately one grasps this fact a contradiction strikes one. Why, if labour is the only ultimate source of wealth, are those who work hardest not necessarily the richest? And why do the rich often do very little work at all and yet remain rich?

Marx explained this contradiction by showing that the wealth of the rich was indeed wealth, and like all wealth, produced by labour, but that in this case the labour involved was done by other people. But this point, though true enough, only half-answered the question. For, after all, in modern societies workers are not slaves, and the rich *pay* those who work for them. If the man who actually does the work of production gets paid for his labour, then is not the man who pays him (call him what you like: the rich man, the owner, the boss) merely offering him something else (money, as a rule) in exchange for the value he has created by his labour?

The snag here can be seen if we ask the question: but why and out of what does the owner pay wages to workers —or, as we say, *employ* them? And then it becomes clear, or so Marx thought, that the reason the owner is prepared to employ workers is that to pay them also pays him. It is 'worth his while' to be an employer. And he has, somehow or other, accumulated wealth which enables him to pay others for their labour. And so the question Marx was asking boiled down to this: 'Why, if labour is the source of value, is it worthwhile for the employer to be an employer?' And the answer he gave was that the wages the employer pays the worker *never* correspond to the value of what the worker produces.

Let us put Marx's theory another way. In the state of affairs that Marx was investigating—a society like modern Britain, or France, or Germany—there was, as in all societies, only one source of value—work; and yet the population was divided into two main classes, those who received wages for their work and those who paid those wages. Where did the second class, those who paid the wages, get the wealth which enabled them to pay wages? From the products produced by those whom they paid. It was, therefore, impossible for them to pay those workers the full value of what they produced. In other words, the employer took the products of the labour of their employees and paid them less than those products were worth. The gap between what the employer paid the worker for his labour and the value of what the worker's labour produced, Marx called 'surplus-value' or profit. Making profit from the labour of other poeple was the process which he called 'exploitation'.

Marx did not say that it was wicked to make profit, though he pointed out that profit is in fact that proportion of their labour which the employer steals from his workers. What he was concerned to show was not that the individual employer was a bad man—he knew quite well that many of the employers, as far as their personal lives were concerned, were kind and pleasant— but that this was how the economic system under which man at present lived, worked. It was pointless, he said, to say the employer ought not to make a profit, for he could not live as an employer without making a profit. To be an employer meant to make profit; if you made insufficient profit you could not, in any case, compete with other employers and you would go out of business.

Equally it was nonsense to talk about a 'fair' profit. Apart from the impossibility of deciding who should judge how much profit was 'fair' ('fair' to whom? To the man who made it or to the man who enabled him to make it?) the system simply did not work like that. For the employer as employer there could be only one law: to make as much profit as possible. It was as pointless to blame the employer for making profit as it would be to blame the tiger for killing its prey. Whether your sympathies lay with the tiger or its prey depended simply on which way you looked at the situation, and from whose point of view.

If you looked at it from the point of view of the employer, you were bound to applaud the successful employer (i.e. the one who made profit successfully). But if you looked at the whole business from the point of view of the worker you *never* reached the point at which the system of profit—or appropriation—became 'fair'. It was always a matter of the theft of the products of one's labour; and a relatively small theft was no more 'moral' than a relatively large one, especially when one realized that the most ruthless employer was indeed the one who made the system work best.

The rich, or owning class, then, lived, according to Marx, through the *exploitation* of the labour of those who had nothing but their labour to sell. This theory of exploitation is basic to Marxist economics. It is not, we should notice, a moral theory, a statement of what *ought* or *ought not* to happen. It is, according to Marx, simply a statement of what *does* happen in a particular form of society, the society he describes as 'capitalism' which he saw as the dominant social system of his time and which Marxists believe is still the form of society in the West.

Why did Marx call this society 'capitalism', and what is the significance of the word?

Capitalist society, he maintained, is a form of society in which the 'means of production' (that is to say, the land, the factories, the mines—the places where wealth is produced) are privately owned by individuals who, just because they *are* the owners, control the way the economic system works. What is peculiar about the owning class in capitalism—as opposed to earlier forms of society—is that their ownership and power depend on their ability to accumulate wealth in the form of capital.

Marx's description of how the capitalist system arose we shall come to in the next chapter. At the moment the important thing is to understand his account of what capitalism is and how it works. Let us consider two terms that have just been used: 'means of production' and 'capital'.

Marx, like all deep thinkers, believed we should not take anything in life for granted. We tend to take the question of production for granted. We sit down to breakfast and seldom think of the almost miraculous amount of human work and thought and organization that have made our breakfast possible. The chair we sit in has been made by someone who has taken years to learn the skills involved in making even the simplest chair. The kettle was boiled on a gas-stove using gas supplied through an intricate maze of pipes running for miles through the city, made by metal-workers, laid out by quite different people, controlled with the greatest care by another set of people in order to keep the pressure right—otherwise breakfast might be ten minutes late and we should either go thirsty or miss the bus which runs according to a time-table in order to fit in with other buses, trains, schools, factories, offices and all. It is only when something goes wrong—some sort of traffic jam at some point in the complicated set-up—that we begin to realize how everything fits together and how dependent we all are on a process which, quite literally, keeps the wheels turning.

This process is what Marx, along with other economists, called *production*. Marx did not believe, it should be said, that men live in order to produce. Production was not to him the object of life; but it was the means of improving life and therefore of supreme importance. It is, moreover, what people spend most of their time doing. If we are not actually producing anything at a particular moment we are, as likely as not, preparing, some way or other, to do so in the future. When we eat we are giving our bodies the necessary sustenance without which they cannot produce energy, mental as well as physical; and human energy is the motive power of production. At school we learn the things necessary to help us contribute to the whole process. All forms of human achievement are linked with this business of producing new products, new theories, new arts, new forms of energy, all serving one vast complicated process of human development. If we think of production as something dull, mechanical, boring—or if we simply take it for granted—we shall not understand either what Marx meant by the word, or why he attached so much importance to it.

The simplest 'means of production' is a tool—the tool man uses to help him dig the ground. In modern, complicated societies the means of production are more complex and involve the activity not of single individuals working alone but of many people working together. A factory, a cotton mill, a coal mine, a power station: these are the typical modern means of production. For production is a process—the very life process of human existence.

This is why the question, 'Who controls the means of production?', was to Marx all-important. For upon its answer depended the very nature of any society. According as to who controls the means of production depends the sort of society you have.

Capitalism—unlike, for example, feudalism—is a system of commodity-production. That is to say, it is an economic system which concentrates on producing goods for exchange, or for sale. If you produce something, say a home-made spade for digging in the garden, simply to satisfy your own needs, not to sell or exchange it, that spade is not a commodity. But if you set up a spade-factory to produce spades for sale, these spades are commodities and you are engaging in commodity-production. It is only when techniques are sufficiently advanced to make commodity-production feasible that the possibility

39

of accumulating capital arises. Very primitive peoples cannot engage in commodity-production because their techniques are so simple and limited that they are obliged to spend their whole time producing for their own needs. They have not yet learned the secrets of such marvellous labour-saving devices as the wheel or the plough, let alone the steam-engine. Sale or exchange for them, if it exists at all, is a minor business, a sideline to make things a bit easier, not the central factor in the set-up they live in. But once commodity-production becomes *general*, once it becomes usual for people to spend their lives producing things (say bicycle-valves or mowing-machines, or for that matter, spades) which would be useless to them unless they could be exchanged, via money, for other things, then a new question arises: How is the production of such commodities to be organized? And so we come back to the same question: Who controls the means of production?

The essence of Marx's economic analysis is that, under capitalism, the economic system is organized for the benefit of those who own capital—the class he called capitalists. It is *their* system. Capital is value which produces profit. It is not a thing, a simple accumulation of wealth, like a pile of treasure. It is wealth accumulated for the purpose of making profit through the exploitation of those who work for wages. Captain Flint's treasure in *Treasure Island* was not in itself capital in Marx's sense: it only became so when Squire Trelawney and the rest got hold of it, brought it back to England, and had the chance then to use it as capitalists. Then, as Stevenson hints at the end of his book, some of the treasure-seekers, like Ben Gunn, squandered their share of the treasure, using it unproductively, while others no doubt transformed it into capital and settled down to live on their investments (i.e. by lending money for interest to other capitalists in order to help them to continue the system of exploitation and profit-making).

Does this mean that the workers—those who live by working for wages—get *nothing* out of capitalism? Of course it does not. Obviously, Marx pointed out, workers would not put up with a system out of which they got nothing at all. They get their wages. And if they band together and form such organizations as trades unions, the workers are in a position to insist that their wages are relatively high. And since the capitalist *needs* workers (for without them he could do nothing), he has a natural interest in keeping them at least relatively healthy and contented, though when there is much more labour to be had than he needs—as, for instance, in under-developed colonial countries, or when there is unemployment— even this consideration scarcely operates. But the main point that Marxist economics makes, is that *in no circumstances* can the capitalist ever afford to pay his workers so much in wages that his profits are seriously interfered with. For if he ceases to make profit he ceases to be able to make his system work. Private profit is the driving force of the whole system, not just because individual capitalists are greedy but in the absolutely basic sense that it is what makes it go on at all.

Marx investigated and analysed almost every aspect of the working of the capitalist system, and his conclusions were formulated most fully in his huge work *Capital*, while particular aspects are dealt with in the essays *Wage-Labour and Capital* and *Value, Price, and Profit*.

Now we will try to summarize some of the most important conclusions which Marx drew from the basic economic analysis of capitalism which he had undertaken. Marxist economics state that:

(1) There is a fundamental and unbridgeable conflict of interest under the capitalist system between the capitalist class who own the means of production and the working class who own nothing but their labour-power which they sell to the capitalists in exchange for wages. Nothing, said Marx, can reconcile these two opposing interests. Put most simply, the situation works out like this. The basic, indisputable economic interest of the worker is to get as high wages as possible. But the basic, indisputable economic interest of the capitalist in order to make profit is to pay as low wages as possible. No amount of economic argument, Marx maintained, could get round this insoluble conflict of interest.

Marx was not, of course, the first economist to point to conflicts of economic interest between different sections of the community. The point about his contribution to the subject was that he insisted that, as long as the capitalist system lasted, these different interests could not be brought together. There was no half-way-house, no compromise acceptable to both capitalists and workers. For since the capitalists lived through exploiting the labour of their employees, they could only do well *at the expense* of the workers. Similarly, the workers could only improve their position, get a larger share of the fruits of their labour, *at the expense* of the capitalists.

(2)   Because there is no limit to the need of the capitalist class for profit there is bound under capitalism to be a constant tendency to search for new means of maintaining profit. As soon as one means of making profit is reduced or excluded, another must be found. When the workers, through their trades unions, become so strong that they insist on an increase of wages (using, for instance, strike action or the threat of it) then some other way of keeping up profits must be found. The capitalist has to look elsewhere to recoup himself, and the most obvious place is overseas, to countries that are less developed economically and where labour is cheap because the trade union movement is as yet not so strong.

Marx believed that this remorseless drive of capitalists for profit and their constant need to find new markets for their products, new sources of cheap labour and new enterprises in which they could profitably invest their money, was what led to the whole system of colonialism and the empires of the capitalist countries. He had no sympathy whatever with the empire-builders and their colonial system. He held that colonies were exploited by the capitalist class of countries like Britain and France and Portugal, not for the benefit of the native peoples but solely for the sake of the profits which the capitalists got out of them. And he believed that this system operated against the interests of the working class in those countries which possessed colonies, for the profits the capitalists made out of the colonies enabled them to keep their system going and therefore to continue to exploit their own workers. This whole system led, in addition, to wars between the different capitalist countries, each trying to grab undeveloped areas of the world to exploit.

(3)   Capitalism is, at its very basis, a competitive economic system, and is for that reason never completely under control, even by the capitalists themselves. You cannot plan a system based on competition any more than you can plan the results of a race. If you do so there is no point in the race and the competitors will not feel inclined to compete. Since the very nature of the capitalist system involves a competitive race for profits among the capitalists it can be subject only to a limited amount of control.

What affects production under capitalism, Marx said, was not a plan worked out by men themselves in order to satisfy the ascertainable needs of humanity, but an impersonal force called 'the market'. A capitalist decides to make such-and-such a product in his factory (say, spades again) not because he knows men are in need of spades, but because he thinks he can get profit by making spades. He does not know whether the supply of spades he and other factory owners will produce corresponds with the actual need for spades of the people; he merely hopes he will be able to beat his competitors and 'capture the market'. But just what the market is—just how many spades society wants at a particular moment—he does not know and has no scientific means of knowing, for his economic system begins, so to speak, from the opposite end. It does not begin by enquiring into human needs and then planning how to satisfy them. It begins with the necessity of making profit and then plans, in so far as it plans at all, how to do that.

Much of the planning capitalist industry goes in for is in fact what we have come to call 'advertisement', that is to say, attempts to persuade people that they 'need' that particular firm's product. Nothing could illustrate better the distinction Marx drew between 'planning for need' and 'planning for profit'. The capitalist begins with his wish to make profit. He then looks round to see how he can make it. Obviously he can sell things to people only if they are prepared to buy them. What the capitalist is interested in is not the real needs of the people but what they can be persuaded to buy. Therefore the capitalist is in the end at the mercy of this thing called 'the market' (i.e. his capacity to sell his products) whose operation is subject to various influences which he cannot accurately predict because the system as a whole is by its very nature unplanned.

This is not an easy point either to explain or grasp because the whole process we are dealing with is a complex one with many sides to it. Perhaps it becomes clearer if we look at it also, as Marx did, from another angle.

When the capitalist system is working well, production is increasing and the capitalist is making a profit. But he can continue to make profit only as long as people go on buying the products his factory produces. Since what he produces is not planned on the basis of what is needed by the people but simply on the basis of hoping he can get rid of it, a time comes when he may not be able to sell his products at a profit. When he runs into economic difficulties (i.e. finds it hard to keep up profits) he can really do only one of two things: he can either increase the price of his products, or pay less to his workers. But whichever of these courses he takes will tend to make matters worse. For either has the effect of making the workers poorer, and the workers are, after all, consumers (the people who buy things) as well as producers (those who make things).

The capitalist is faced, then, with a kind of vicious circle. He produces commodities as though there were no limit to the demand for them, yet the wages system on which capitalism operates limits the market all the time. Because he produces for profit, the capitalist will always tend in the end, from his point of view, to produce more than he can get rid of, and the economic crisis which this leads to is invariably made worse by the very measures he takes to try to solve it.

This is why Marx stressed the tendency of capitalism as an economic system not to develop smoothly but to move all the time from boom (a period in which the system is working well) to crisis (in which there is a halt or even a reversal in the increase in production, a tendency to unemployment and a reduction in living standards).

Marx always emphasized, incidentally, that what capitalists call over-production, that is to say, the state of not being able to get rid of their products profitably, is not really over-production in the sense that more is being produced than the people need or can do with. What the people actually need for their steady, balanced, all-round development is never considered.

To sum up then: Marx called the economic system which he saw in existence 'capitalism', and pointed to its chief characteristic as the ownership of the means of production by private individuals whom he described as capitalists. He maintained that the basis and driving-force of capitalism was the need of the capitalist to make profit, and his analysis of profit or surplus-value led him to conclude that profit was always and could only be made at the expense of the workers, who sold their labour-power to the capitalists for wages. He saw, as a result, a number of contradictions embedded deep in the very nature of the capitalist system. The chief of these were:

(a) A complete and unbridgeable conflict of interest between the capitalist owners on the one side and the wage-earning workers on the other, neither class being able to improve its position save at the expense of the other.

(b) A contradiction between what he called the 'social nature' of modern production (i.e. the fact that it involved the constant co-operation of many people, all doing particular, specialized jobs) and the private ownership of the actual means of production.

(c) A competitiveness, inherent in the system, which led individual capitalists into constant conflict with one another and capitalist nations into an international trade-race and ultimately war.

(d) An inability to plan the economy on the basis of the people's needs, and instead an inevitable tendency towards periodic economic crisis.

CHAPTER 2

MARX AND HISTORY

As WE have seen, Karl Marx claimed that his description of capitalist society was entirely objective, that is to say, strictly in accordance with all the facts. Nevertheless, he did not of course deny that the picture he gave of that society was highly critical and indeed a damning one.

Marx was not the only man of his time to say damning things about capitalism and the way it worked. In England alone during Marx's lifetime such writers as Carlyle, Ruskin and Dickens, to say nothing of the Chartist leaders, built up an extremely critical case against existing society. Yet Marx went even further than these other opponents of things as they were, and one of the principal reasons he was able to do so and to found what has turned out to be the most universal revolutionary movement mankind has known, was that, unlike these others, he and Engels went deeply into the questions: Why and how did the present society arise? How does history, as a process, operate? Are there such things as historical laws?

Why, it may well be asked, should a revolutionary need a theory of history? Surely it was the future rather than the past that the founder of communism might be expected to concentrate on? Yet Marx's work contains comparatively few detailed discussions about what future society will be like, and the most full and elaborate analysis of what has happened in the past. Why?

The answer is in fact a fairly simple one. Perhaps the most revolutionary of all the things Marx said about capitalism was that it had not always existed, and that therefore it would be most unnatural if it were to exist for ever. This idea—very largely owing to the influence of Marx himself—sounds less startling today than it did a hundred years ago. Then it was almost universally assumed that what the classical economists like Adam Smith and Ricardo called the laws of economics were true then and forever. Marx agreed that many of the economic laws in question were indeed true, but he added the important phrase, as long as capitalism exists.

Now the point here is that every unjust society always has its critics; and when that society is as blatantly unjust as early industrial capitalism was to the poor, these criticisms are often violent and passionate. Men feel bitterly hostile to things as they are. But if they also believe that the evils they hate are more or less inevitable, springing from the natural sinfulness of man or from certain iron laws of economics which no one can alter, then this takes the edge off their criticisms and even their feelings. For if society has always been like that— if there has always been exploitation and the rich have always lived on the labour of the poor—then, however unpleasant this may be, it is unlikely that anyone will ever be able to do much about it.

Hence, alongside the critical, angry ideas, another sort of idea develops, often in the same man's head, which does much to counteract the criticism. People say, 'Exploitation is unjust', but they also say, 'The poor are always with us; it's always been like that and I suppose it always will be'. They say, 'It's a scandal that there should be poverty amidst plenty', but they also say, 'But you can't change human nature'. They say, 'These conditions are intolerable', but they also say, 'Well, you have to put up with things and make the best of a bad job'. And each time the second sentence all but cancels out the first.

It did not take a man like Marx to convince men and women who worked for fourteen hours a day for a miserable wage and never had a summer holiday that they were badly off. What Marx had to convince them was that it was possible to do something about it. And the first point he made was that capitalism was not a God-given or eternal form of society, corresponding to some unalterable dispensation of nature, but one particular form of human society which had arisen at a particular time for reasons which could be clearly explained, and which, far from being unchangeable, was constantly changing and indeed contained within itself the seeds of its own decay. Marx was able to make this point and back it up because, besides being an economist, he was a historian. For he and Engels developed a theory of history just as important as Darwin's theory of evolution that revolutionized men's understanding of the biological sciences.

Marx asked the question: How did capitalist society come into existence? And the answer he gave was that it came into being as the capitalist class became the dominant class in society. The early capitalists were merchants. In Britain during the Middle Ages the merchants played an important part in the life of the nation, but not the dominant part. The rulers at this time were not the merchants but the landowners; and in this—the feudal era—the landowners' power did not depend on their development of the productive wealth of the soil but on the brute fact that they received enforced services, in the form of labour, produce, rent, and military services, from their tenants. A feudal baron stayed rich not because his investments were bringing in a high interest, but because he was strong and independent enough to tyrannize over his tenants and squeeze every possible ounce of service from them. The feudal ruling class, Marx argued, did not owe their power to the accumulation of wealth in the form of capital. This was why they were not particularly interested in the improvement of techniques of production or indeed in scientific development at all. During the whole feudal period there was less technical advance—fewer mechanical discoveries or improvements in methods of agriculture—than in any fifty years of capitalist society.

But even under feudalism the merchants gradually came to play a more important part in the economy of the country. They became more and more prosperous. The towns, instead of being mere occasional oases among the feudal estates, had become by the 16th century the vital and developing centres of life. And the merchants lived in the towns or travelled from one town to another. They were called burghers because they lived in the burghs or boroughs, and this is the origin of the French word *bourgeois* which Marx used to describe the merchant or capitalist class. *Bourgeoisie* simply meant, originally, townsmen; the point Marx stressed was that the whole way of life of the town-dwelling merchants was different from that of the feudal landowners, for they lived by the accumulation of money-wealth and the manufacture and sale of commodities. They imported wine from France and Spain, exported wool to Holland, and trained apprentices in the skills and tricks of their particular craft. They had in fact the essential characteristics of capitalists, and capitalism came into existence as the merchant class gradually became as important as the class of feudal landowners, and finally overthrew them as the dominant power in society.

The story of the way the capitalist class superseded the feudal nobility as the ruling class in Western Europe, Marx called the 'bourgeois revolution'. It was, he pointed out, a revolution which took place at different dates in different countries. England and Holland, the centres of the medieval wool trade, were the first predominantly capitalist countries in the world. The key event of the bourgeois revolution in England was the civil war of the 17th century and the victory of the Parliamentary forces which represented the new power of the capitalist class, concentrated especially in London and East Anglia, where sheep-farming for profit had displaced the old feudal forms of agriculture. Up to 1640 the dominant class in England was the feudal nobility; after 1649 it was the capitalist merchants. Of course to put it in this way over-simplifies what Marx showed to be a long and very complicated struggle; but it expresses the essence of it.

Capitalism, then, according to Marx, came into existence when the merchants and manufacturers and bankers—the capitalist class—had carried through a revolution which put them in control of society and enabled them to shape that society according to their needs and interests. It was fundamentally an *economic* revolution, a change in the way production was organized. But the bourgeois revolution was not only an economic revolution—it also involved a political revolution and a revolution in ideas. For the capitalist class, in order to build up a capitalist society, had to take over control not only of the economy of the country but also of the State —the organization of government. This was why the bourgeois revolutions in both England and France involved chopping off the head of the old-type king (the feudal ruler) and establishing the authority of new forms of government—Parliaments. And in the course of the revolution the capitalist class also had to encourage and develop new ways of thinking, ways appropriate to the new society.

The most important of the new ideas which took hold of men's minds at the time of the bourgeois revolution and during the period of capitalism was the idea of *individualism*—that each individual is a completely separate independent creature working out his own salvation on his own—an idea which corresponded to the form production under capitalism took, the individual producer owning his property and developing it as a profit-making concern in competition with other business-men. This individualist way of looking at things had its good side: it gave men like Luther and Cranmer and other Protestants the courage to stand out against the authority of the old feudal world. But it also led to an attitude to freedom well expressed in the phrase 'Each for himself and the devil take the hindmost', or as it is put today 'I'm all right, Jack'.

The bourgeois revolution which in country after country ushered in the capitalist system, and in much of Europe was still taking place during Marx's lifetime, was, then, the culmination of a struggle for power between two classes—the feudal landowners and the capitalist merchants. And it was one of the main points about Marx's view of history that such struggles were not something exceptional but were taking place all the time. 'The history of all hitherto existing society is the history of class struggles', wrote Marx and Engels in *The Communist Manifesto*. It is the most famous and perhaps the most important of all their statements about history.

Marx has often been accused by his opponents of preaching or encouraging class struggle. His answer was that it was not the communists who invented the class struggle but the society they were born into. The class struggle existed and would always exist as long as society was divided into classes with opposing interests. Marx did not say the class struggle was something desirable; he said it was something real, which had to be recognized.

When they wrote, 'The history of all hitherto existing society is the history of class struggles', Marx and Engels were referring to *written* history, that is to say, the history of the last few thousand years. They did not hold that classes, in the sense they always used the word, have always existed, as Engels makes clear in his book *The Origin of the Family*. A class, in the Marxist sense, is a group of people who stand in a common relationship to the means of production. The capitalist class is a class because all who belong to it are owners of productive enterprises who live by exploiting the labour of those they employ. What makes a person a member of the working class is not that he works or that he is comparatively poor. Shopkeepers often work very hard, but they are not members of the working class. A bankrupt business-man may be poor, but until he begins to work for wages he is not a member of the working class. Peasants or smallholders (there are not many of them in Britain today, but in some countries there are millions) who own and work on their own plot of land, are often poor and nearly always work immensely hard, but Marx did not classify them as members of the working class. What makes a worker a worker is that he sells his labour-power for wages.

In primitive, tribal societies such as all men lived in up to about four thousand years ago there were not, at any rate at first, classes. As we saw in the last chapter, Marx pointed out that the main characteristic of primitive society is that men have not yet learned how to produce much more than what they need, their simple personal requirements. There is no commodity-production on a large scale for sale or exchange, for there is as yet very little division of labour, except perhaps within individual families. Therefore, although primitive societies may produce leaders—the strongest and most skilful men—and other individuals, like witch-doctors, who because of their real or imagined cleverness have a special authority among the tribe, they do not produce class divisions until such a time as the people have learned how to produce a surplus above their immediate needs. When that time comes—and again we have already touched on Marx's argument previously—the question arises: Who is to control that surplus and its production?

The class struggle, as Marx described it, is at bottom the struggle for the control of the surplus produced by men as their technical skills and ability to invent machinery increase. Classes arose because in the course of technical advance it became possible for a section of the people to get control of the productive processes and develop them *for their own benefit, their own profit*, not for the common good of all.

Marx did not pass a moral judgment on the fact that power over the productive processes had passed into the hands of a class and that society had thenceforth been divided. He thought that it was probable that only through such a process, through the appearance of a comparatively-leisured ruling class, men could in fact have made the discoveries that freed them from the limitations of primitive society. Marx did not therefore pass judgment on the historical fact that classes had come into existence. He did, however, pour scorn on the idea that the division was caused either by the natural greed or inborn sinfulness of man and was therefore due to some eternal unchanging aspect of human nature. Class divisions, he insisted, had come about through a perfectly understandable social process at a certain stage in the development of human society. They were neither God-given nor eternal, and certainly not due to any inborn division of mankind into the 'natural' rulers and the 'natural' slaves.

Within a society that is divided into classes with fundamentally different interests there is bound, Marx maintained, to be a struggle between those classes. It did not follow, of course, that this struggle was at all times equally violent or even that it was obvious. The class struggle went on even when everything appeared on the surface to be calm. It went on even when those taking part in it were not conscious of doing so. Indeed, most men (especially members of exploited classes) were conscious of the class struggle only at moments of social crisis. For one of the important features of the class struggle was that the ruling class always tried to pretend that it did not exist and that those who said it did were simply trouble-makers trying to upset everything.

Marx and Engels did not suggest that the class struggle was a simple business, a straight fight between goodies and baddies. If it had been, they recognized, it would have been over long ago. It is the essence of their conception of the class struggle that though, at bottom, the issues are clear, they have been so overgrown with complications and false ideas that the struggle is in fact very seldom fought out straightforwardly or with naked weapons. Not only this, but class society (which is how Marx described societies which are divided into classes) has itself had a sufficiently complicated history. All class societies are not alike.

Within the era of class society, Marx distinguished between three main periods or types of society—slave society, feudal society, and capitalist society. He did not say that all countries necessarily passed through all three stages, or that each stage lasted the same length of time in the history of different societies. Nevertheless, the three main stages corresponded to definite stages in man's economic and social advance, and the class struggle during these different stages took different forms. We have already seen how Marx described the struggle between the feudal and capitalist classes which resulted in the bourgeois revolution and the establishing of modern capitalist society. It is worth making two points in particular about this.

In the first place, Marx believed that in this conflict the capitalist class was a *progressive* force. That is to say, he believed that in Britain in the 16th and 17th centuries as in other countries later, it was necessary for general human development that feudal society should be ended. Feudal society, which in its day had itself had its progressive sides, was by this time holding back the possible advances of which men were now capable—great advances in the mastery of nature and the development of new human productive abilities. The feudal ruling class was afraid of scientific progress lest such progress undermined the ideas about the world which helped preserve feudalism. This was why, for instance, the official Papal astronomers refused to look through Galileo's telescope: they were afraid that what they saw would prove that the earth went round the sun instead of vice versa, and that, if this new fact were established, all the theology of the day would be undermined. Such attitudes made the ending of feudal society essential if mankind were to advance at all. And the only people in Britain in the 16th and 17th centuries capable of overthrowing feudalism and replacing it by a more productive form of society were the merchant class. Therefore it was historically necessary for capitalism at this point to replace feudalism as the form of British society. And the bourgeois revolution was therefore something progressive, helpful to general human progress at the time when it took place.

In the second place, although the bourgeois revolution was in this important sense progressive, the new society it brought into being was, just as definitely as feudalism, a class society. The prosperous business-men who welcomed the execution of Charles I and were busy developing the trade routes to India formed a new, privileged ruling class. Therefore the bourgeois revolution, though necessary in its day, merely meant the replacement of one exploiting class by another. Instead of being ground down by the feudal nobles, the mass of the people were now exploited by the business-men who ran the capitalist system. All revolutions within the framework of class society, Marx maintained, were of this kind. They might involve necessary advances in the processes of production, but they did not solve or end the contradictions which existed in *all* class societies. They did not end the class struggle but merely altered its form.

It is important to grasp these points because they help us to understand a very deep thought which was always in Marx's mind when he talked about the history of mankind. It is this: that although human history during the last two or three thousand years has been the history of warring classes, each fighting for its own interests, yet there is also to be divined within this often cruel and sordid story, something which can genuinely be called human progress—a movement towards a society which is not just *different* from previous societies but *higher*, more in line with people's deepest needs and hopes and possibilities.

The picture of historical development that Marx and Engels painted is the picture of successive brutal struggles for power. Much less than other historians do they see history as a steady, fairly peaceful process inspired by beautiful thoughts and splendid ideals. The satisfaction of material needs they emphasize as fundamental, involving men's vital energies. Yet it would be quite misleading to infer from this emphasis on down-to-earth struggles for existence that Marx's view of history was a cynical or sordid one, never rising above the lowest of human motives and appetites. On the contrary, Marx and Engels were fervent believers in human progress and the power of men and women to rise to the most splendid heroism and noble achievements. For alongside the history of a succession of class societies in each of which the principal aim of the ruling class was to keep their own particular system of exploitation going, they saw another story. This was the story of the age-long attempts of the common people gradually to acquire more and more

Frederick Engels

Marx and Engels, with Marx's three daughters, Eleanor, Jenny, and Laura

control of their own destinies, more control over nature through science, more control over society through the extension of democracy.

And this inspiring story, rich in adventurous ideas and selfless sacrifice—the story of John Ball and Jack Cade, of the New Model Army in the Civil War, of the French Revolution with its slogan of 'Liberty, Equality, Fraternity', of the great Chartist movement and its successor the modern socialist movement—this Marx told with intense feeling and a sense of pride. Nor is it only the revolutionary heroes and martyrs who emerge from Marxist history as the standard-bearers of human progress. Because he saw the class struggle not simply as a sordid battle for self-interest but as a part of human development as a whole, Marx was able to recognize the progressive part played at certain times even by men and women who belonged to exploiting classes. Marx and Engels did not agree with many of the views of Joan of Arc or Luther or Oliver Cromwell or Milton or George Washington or Robespierre or Shelley; but they saw such men and women as contributing nobly to the advance of humanity. And the contribution of the scientists like Bacon and Boyle and Newton they saw as sheer human gain.

It is the combination of realistic, down-to-earth analysis of the material, economic basis of things with a passionate feeling for human advance and achievement that gives Marx's view of history its great power and his actual historical writings like *The Civil War in France* their remarkable punch and vividness.

But the idea of progress which Marxist history so passionately expresses is not a simple, automatic, continuous sort of progress. Marx certainly did not believe that all is for the best in the best of all possible worlds, or that human beings build a better world simply by having noble and enlightened thoughts. Marx's view of history is a revolutionary view in the sense that he thought that history proved that human advances came through struggle and conflict which at certain points involve revolutionary changes in the way society is organized.

By a revolution he did not mean necessarily a change that involved bloodshed. Some revolutions were violent, others could be peaceful. But a revolution always meant a fundamental change in the class structure of society. The bourgeois revolution was a revolutionary change because it involved the taking of essential power out of the feudal class and the establishing of the capitalist class as the force controlling the economy and the state. Every revolution, Marx insisted, was by its very nature always opposed by the class that stood to lose power and privilege. Yet revolutions were necessary and, if humanity were to progress to higher and more productive forms of society, inevitable.

It is stupid, Marx held, to be afraid of the idea of revolution, just as it is stupid to be afraid of the idea of class struggle. In class-divided societies a class struggle is inevitable and revolution is the natural, inevitable way of progress. Not to understand this was not to understand history.

CHAPTER 3

THE REVOLUTIONARY

KARL MARX was a revolutionary because, as we have seen, he came to believe that history was itself a series of revolutions and that any thoroughgoing change in the nature of the society of his time would mean a revolution. He was not a romantic sort of revolutionary carrying a bomb in his pocket or imagining that the world could be improved by acts of terrorism or assassination. Indeed, he spent a great deal of his time arguing against the anarchists of his day who did believe in that kind of thing. Marx thought that despite their sincerity they were hopelessly unrealistic and did the real revolutionary movement more harm than good.

Marx was a revolutionary because he could not accept the capitalist system as the best possible form of social organization for the modern world. On the contrary, as we already know, he saw it as a thoroughly wasteful and inefficient system which had outlived its usefulness. The essence of his case against capitalism was that it was hindering the progress of mankind. For he had come to the conclusion that by its very nature capitalism was incapable of solving the actual problems facing modern man, or allowing them to be solved. Among the chief of these were the problems of using and planning to the full the enormous resources modern science had opened up, the problem of ending wars and enabling men to co-operate instead of compete with each other, the problem of ending the poverty and injustice brought about by economic exploitation.

It would, however, be wrong to emphasize only these sides of Marx's case against capitalism, for they tend perhaps to stress its inefficiency and unscientific nature rather than its human defects. Marx was a humanist. He believed passionately in the dignity of human beings and their capacity to improve themselves and their lot. He was not an efficiency expert bent on making things work more smoothly without regard for human values. If he grew indignant about the inefficiency of capitalism and attacked it as a monstrously unscientific system, it was because he believed that this inefficiency prevented human beings from fulfilling their inmost needs and putting into practice the ideals and principles they most valued. Marx did not worship science for its own sake but honoured it because he saw it as man's chief means of mastering nature and improving the human condition.

Therefore we should add to Marx's specific criticisms of capitalism the most fundamental criticism of all: that it was preventing, in his judgment, men and women from becoming more free. Free above all to develop their individual abilities to the maximum, free to live the kind of life they quite rightly and realistically wanted. And it is important to include women as well as men in the last two sentences. Marx considered women to be the worst sufferers from the system of exploitation, and he emphasized time and again that a revolutionary change would involve as one of its chief consequences the possibility of the full emancipation of women.

Marx began his political activities, as we saw in Part One, as a critic and reformer who wanted to help make the world better but had no very definite convictions or programme, beyond the conviction that you can begin to change anything only if you have first discovered exactly how it works at present. He became a revolutionary through his practical experience of capitalist governments and his analysis of the way capitalism worked. And from the age of about twenty-eight he called himself a communist, doing more than any other single man to found the modern communist movement.

The word communist has gathered round itself in the last hundred years so many emotions, so many prejudices and so much controversy, that one has to make a conscious and rather difficult effort if one is to try to examine fairly calmly and objectively what the word signifies.

The key idea behind the word is that of a society in which private profit has been abolished and where everything is organized for the common benefit. It was not an idea that began with Karl Marx. Three hundred years earlier the Englishman Sir Thomas More had outlined the idea in his book *Utopia*. It must have been fairly familiar to the Elizabethans, and Shakespeare in *The*

Tempest makes old Gonzalo speak of his imaginary society or commonwealth of the future:

> All things in common Nature should produce
> Without sweat or endeavour: treason, felony,
> Sword, pike, knife, gun, or need of any engine
> Would I not have: but Nature should bring forth
> Of its own kind, all foison*, all abundance
> To feed my innocent people.

Less than a hundred years later, at the time of the Civil War, several of the groups on the Parliamentary side—especially the Levellers and the Diggers—were contributing in rather more practical terms to the development of similar ideas. Later, during the French Revolution, the left-wing among the revolutionaries contained men like Babeuf who had communist ideas.

The main point, however, to be made about these early visions of communism (at least before Babeuf) is that in the nature of things they were indeed visions, utopias, dreams of a different sort of society, far removed from any possibility of actually coming about. They express men's hopes and ideals, but not within the realm of practical politics. They were, therefore, though persistently cropping up in the thoughts and hopes of individuals, without much real influence, though it is interesting to notice that it was at critical moments of the bourgeois revolution (see page 52) that these ideas became for the first time practical forces. The Levellers and the Diggers were defeated fairly easily; Babeuf less easily.

* The same word as the French *foisson*, 'harvest'.

But they were, unlike Gonzalo, a real force. By the time of the next wave of bourgeois revolutions in 1848 such ideas were even stronger, especially among the workers of Paris, Vienna, London, and the north of England. And it was in 1848 that *The Communist Manifesto* was published.

The ferment of ideas and plans which filled the air at the critical moments in which the capitalist class was struggling to carry through *its* revolution, included ideas which went much further in the revolutionary direction than the capitalists were prepared to go. A Marxist would say there were two reasons for this. In the first place, revolutions of any kind, just because they *are* revolutions, put ideas into people's heads. The capitalist class, by carrying through the destruction of feudal society, demonstrated that things as they were were not eternal, that men could in fact change the world—and this was an important lesson. In the second place, the capitalist class, in order to carry through its revolution successfully, needed the help of people who were not themselves capitalists. The New Model Army was the principal weapon of the capitalist class in the English Civil War; but not all the soldiers of the New Model Army were capitalists. In other words, in the course of freeing themselves from feudal rule and feudal ideas the capitalist class willy-nilly also changed the lives and outlooks of many humbler people, workers, small shopkeepers, small producers and peasant-farmers. The ideas and, to some extent, the practice of democracy grew. And all this greatly strengthened the *independent* ideas which the common people were able to develop on their own behalf —especially the most revolutionary of all such ideas: that perhaps society could get along without capitalists.

But beneath the growth of ideas which pointed towards communism there was, according to Marx's approach to these matters, something more fundamental. As we have seen, Marx was convinced that the force which really moved history was not an idea but the way people lived and produced. He had shown how it was impossible to get rid of the feudal system, for all its injustice and out-of-date ideas, until another class arose capable of taking power out of the hands of the feudal nobles. It was merely an extension of this argument to insist that the capitalist system, however unsatisfactory it might be, would not be got rid of until a class had arisen capable of taking power out of the hands of the capitalists.

It was, in fact, not until capitalism had reached a fairly late stage of development—the stage ushered in by the Industrial Revolution and the beginning of really large-scale industry of the sort we are now familiar with—that a class arose, according to Marx, capable of taking power out of the hands of the capitalist class and founding a different sort of society. This class was the modern working class.

There had of course been wage-earning workers before the Industrial Revolution, but they could scarcely as yet form an effective or self-conscious class. For one thing, they were too dispersed: few enterprises employed more than a score or two of workers. For another, the nature of their employment prevented most of them from

Marx's house in London: 1 Modena Villas, Maitland Park Road

(*Above*) 'Karl Marx gives a lecture', from a painting by N. N. Schukov.

(*Left*) Marx's tomb in Highgate Cemetery

developing the consciousness of being members of a strong independent class. The vast army of servants in the 18th century—the cooks and valets and parlourmaids and skivvies—were wage-earners, and their wages were little enough. But they were not wage-earners engaged in production and therefore able to feel that, if only they received all the fruits of their labour, they could be strong and independent. On the contrary, they tended to feel, as personal servants always tend to, that if there were no masters and ladies there would be no work.

What changed the whole situation, then, was the development of large-scale industry and the appearance of the great new manufacturing towns like Manchester and Leeds and Sheffield and Birmingham. For these towns—and London itself—became the centres of a new sort of working class (Marx often referred to it as the 'proletariat'), a class of industrial workers, massed together by the very nature of the factories and towns, living often in the most atrocious conditions, and more systematically exploited than any previous body of workers.

Marx in *Capital* and Engels in his *Condition of the Working Class in England in 1844* have left unforgettable accounts of the wretched way of life of the working class in the early stages of Industrial Capitalism. But they always maintained that it was not primarily the poverty of the workers or the ghastly conditions in which they lived—including of course child-labour as an accepted part of the system—that made the industrial workers a revolutionary class. Poverty and bad conditions are just as likely to make people hopeless as to turn them into revolutionaries. What gave the new working class the possibility of becoming a revolutionary class capable of overthrowing the capitalist system was (i) they worked in the factories and mills and mines at the very point of production and were therefore able to become fully conscious of what economic exploitation meant—they could *see* they were being robbed; (ii) the very nature of their work—massed together in large factories—and taking part in a form of production in which each person involved clearly depended on the others—made them able to learn the importance of solidarity and co-operation; (iii) because of these two facts they were capable of envisaging a different sort of society in which there were no capitalists or owners; and they had every reason to desire such a society. That is why Marx and Engels ended *The Communist Manifesto* with the slogan, 'Workers of the world, unite!' and added the sentence, 'You have nothing to lose but your chains'.

You cannot make a revolution unless you are clear as to the sort of society you want in place of the existing one. Marx did not see the working-class revolution simply as a means of destruction; he saw it as the means of establishing a new form of society which he called *communism*. And he argued that the first, necessary step towards communism was to replace capitalism by a kind of society called socialism. The revolution at which Marx and Engels and their followers aimed was to be a *socialist revolution*.

Socialism, said Marx—echoing other socialist thinkers

of his time—is a society in which the working class has taken power out of the hands of the capitalists and organizes the economy of the country for the benefit of all instead of for the profit of the few. Under socialism the means of production—all the major industries and the land—are no longer owned by private individuals but are publicly owned. In practice this means they are run by the state which is itself responsible to and controlled by the producers themselves—the working class.

Marx, it should be noticed, was not advocating 'state-control' or 'nationalization' for its own sake. The important question to him was: What kind of state did the controlling? Who, in fact, ran the nationalized industries? If it was a capitalist state, still controlled by the capitalist class, it would, even if it took over control of certain industries, still run them for the benefit of the capitalist system and its need for profits. Therefore the important thing about socialism was that the state itself should be taken over by the working class and the power of the exploiting class completely broken.

There could be no compromise about this. Whether the socialist revolution was accomplished quickly or slowly, with violence or peacefully (and Marx himself believed that in Britain, for instance, the revolution could be a peaceful one), the main thing was that it should be thorough. You cannot, Marx taught, have two ruling classes: you cannot build socialism without destroying capitalism and you cannot end capitalism without taking all power out of the hands of the capitalists and those who support their system.

71

The socialist revolution, Marx said, would be by far the most important revolution in the entire history of humanity. For whereas all previous revolutions had resulted in the transfer of power from one exploiting class to another, from feudal nobles to capitalist business-men for instance, the socialist revolution would bring in a society in which *all* class exploitation would come to an end. The class struggle which for centuries had dominated human history would be brought to an end through the triumph of the working class. For the working class alone could establish a society in which classes would be abolished. The capitalist class—or any exploiting class—could never in the nature of things do this, for since to be a capitalist means to get profit from the work of others, you cannot possibly have a society in which all men are capitalists. But you *can* have a society in which all men are workers. That is why, Marx maintained, the working class, despite all its apparent disadvantages, is in the long run stronger than the capitalist class. For whereas the capitalist class can never do without the working class, the workers can get on perfectly well without capitalists. And this, Marx and Engels said, is the only way of ending class struggle. The working class takes economic and political power away from the capitalists. 'The expropriators are expropriated.'

Socialism, said Marx, is in the essential sense a classless society, for the power of any section of the community to exploit economically and to gain profit through the work of other people has been abolished. This does not mean of course that Marx believed that suddenly, overnight, with the socialist revolution all human problems would be automatically solved. In one sense, and an important one, the problems were just beginning. For the new feature of socialist society was not that social problems would not arise, but that they could be solved. Under capitalism, for instance, you could not solve the problem of preventing war, because capitalism, by its very nature and structure, tended towards war. Under socialism, however, it became possible to do away with wars because the basic conflicts of interest which caused wars no longer existed.

This did not mean that even in a completely socialist world it would necessarily be easy to prevent war, for socialism would not automatically smooth out all disagreements or do away with all the old ways of thinking. Marx and Engels did not offer a guarantee that within a few years of the establishment of socialism there would be no corrupt practices in society, like trying to feather one's own nest by living as a spiv: they did not offer a guarantee that within a few years there would be no colour prejudice. What they said was that in a class society like capitalism you cannot stamp out spivs however much you want to, for the idea of trying to get something for nothing is embedded in the very workings of capitalism: it is what capitalists themselves do. Similarly, you cannot stamp out colour prejudice so long as the people of Africa and Asia are being used as cheap labour under capitalism. Whereas in a socialist society such practices and ideas are no longer necessary and can therefore be changed, though changing them will be difficult.

Marx was convinced that those people who had a privileged position under capitalism would do everything in their power to try to prevent and resist the coming of socialism. This, he pointed out, had always been the case in previous revolutions. Slave owners had not permitted the abolition of slavery without a fight. Capitalists were not likely to welcome the end of their system. It was not simply that ruling classes were greedy; they had sincerely convinced themselves that the destruction of their system would be a terrible tragedy. For every ruling class, Marx taught, builds up ideas and moral principles which they think of as being objectively and even eternally true, but which are really mere justifications of their own privileges. To the capitalist the idea of freedom involves free enterprise, the right to make profits by exploiting other people. He therefore believes that a society in which exploitation is illegal is less free than one in which it is permitted. So when the capitalist class fights to protect its privileges and opposes the introduction of socialism it always does so in the name of freedom—even though in fact the introduction of socialism will mean more freedom for more people.

Did Marx believe that under socialism there would be complete equality, equal wages for all? No, he did not. Marxist thinking about socialism stresses that it is a society based on the common ownership of the means of production and run on the principle, 'From each according to his ability: to each according to his work'. Each person contributes to society according to his skill and willingness. And he gets paid according to the value of his work to society. If society at a particular stage particularly needs responsible engineers, then responsible engineers will tend to get particularly high wages. In other words, financial incentives are still used, though in a planned way and for the general benefit. There will not, however, ever be under socialism anything like the same inequality of income that prevails in capitalist society; and—the vital point—even those who earn most under socialism cannot use their money to exploit others, cannot own a factory or invest on the stock exchange.

This last paragraph illustrates why Marx made an important distinction between socialism and communism. Socialism he saw as the necessary transition-stage between class society and communist society. The socialist revolution was the key event in that transition; yet it did not lead automatically or immediately to the introduction of communism. What it did was to end class society and establish the working class as the ruling force in the new society. Whereas by the time of communism, classes would have entirely disappeared, in the period of socialism the working class would act as a new kind of ruling class, not in the sense of *exploiting* any other class but in the sense of consolidating the revolution and preventing any attempts, either from disgruntled ex-capitalists at home or by their friends abroad, to overthrow the new society. It was, above all, the experiences of the Paris Commune which led Marx, in his later life, to stress this point.

The questions of the actual way the socialist revolution would be carried through and how socialism would be transformed into communism were not discussed in great detail by Marx. This was because he was very much of a realist in his thinking and did not believe it to be possible to deal with a situation in advance, except in general terms. It was later Marxists of the period of the socialist revolution itself—particularly Lenin—who developed this side of Marx's thoughts. Yet on the general pattern of development Marx's ideas are clear. They can be summarized as follows:

(1)   The socialist revolution is the natural consequence of the development of human society in the era of class struggle, and it is inevitable in the sense that *only* in this way can men advance to a higher stage of society in which they are free to solve their present problems.

(2)   Capitalism can be ended and the socialist revolution successfully achieved only by the action of the working class. In carrying through the socialist revolution, however, the working class acts not only in its own interest but in the interest of all humanity, for the socialist revolution ends class society for ever and abolishes the exploitation of man by man. In this way the class struggle is resolved and the whole people once again get control of the surplus which they produce. A new era in human history begins.

(3)   Socialism, the form of society immediately ushered in by the socialist revolution, is a transitional form of society, between class society and communism, in which the remnants of class division are gradually done away with and the foundations of a classless society laid. Socialism is based on the public ownership of the means of

production and the social principle, 'From each according to his ability: to each according to his work'.

(4)   To carry through the socialist revolution the working class needs to be (*a*) conscious of its power and of its historical role, and (*b*) organized as a political party. It is the job of the communists to provide this consciousness and this leadership. The communist party is therefore a new type of party. As the *Communist Manifesto* puts it: 'They have no interests separate and apart from those of the working class as a whole.' Without the existence of a communist party and its winning of power the socialist revolution is impossible.

(5)   Especially in the early days of socialist society the control of the state by the working class and its party is of supreme importance. Otherwise the new society is liable to be overthrown by the old ruling-class forces, helped by their friends and allies abroad. Also, it is only through a firm control of the new state that old ways of behaviour can be gradually changed and foundations of the new classless society firmly laid.

(6)   The socialist revolution is different from previous revolutions in two essential ways. It does not replace one exploiting class by another but abolishes classes altogether. And it is international. The communist movement unites all men everywhere.

(7)   Once the foundations of a classless society have been laid and the new socialist state set on its way, entirely new possibilities of human progress emerge. Because exploitation has been abolished an enormous flood of human energy is released. This new creative energy,

unhampered by the *contradictions* which capitalism imposes (see page 47), enables science and production to soar to undreamt-of heights. An economy of abundance becomes possible in which the needs of all mankind can be satisfied. And this production of abundance both allows and demands the introduction of a social system more radically different from class society than even socialism. Communism becomes possible.

* * * * *

The principle behind communist society will be, 'From each according to his ability, to each according to his need'. Notice the difference between this and the socialist principle. Under socialism people are to be rewarded or paid—repaid perhaps expresses it best—according to the nature of their work. Certain jobs will, for particular social reasons, still carry certain privileges. The doctor or the ballet-dancer will be likely to be paid a good deal more than the engine-driver. There will still be quite a lot of competitiveness and quite a lot of inequality, even though the power to exploit—the most fatal aspect of competitiveness and inequality—has been done away with.

But after a time it will be possible, Marx held, to carry the socialist revolution a stage further and to do away with competitiveness and inequality altogether. This can, however, only become a serious possibility when production has enormously increased and society is able to provide an abundance of human necessities. Then, when so much is being produced that the needs of all, without exception, can be satisfied, the material basis of a communist society exists. Under communism, Marxists anticipate, most essentials of life—housing, basic foods, local transport, and all medicines—will be free, just as, for example, water is practically free in most parts of the world today. The fact that there is an abundance of water prevents people having to compete for it: they have, quite simply, what they need. It may be necessary to take steps to prevent a few people wasting water and at times of drought you may even have to ration it all round; but these are not terribly difficult problems. Obviously Marx did not think a communist society would immediately be able to produce so much of everything that people would be able to satisfy their every need by simply turning a tap on. But he saw no reason why society should not be able to produce sufficient to satisfy everyone's basic requirements and then, from that basic minimum, gradually increase the standard of living of all.

In this way the well-being of the whole people could be steadily improved without society being geared to profit-making and personal go-getting. Marx believed that, in capitalist society, one could only 'get on' at the expense of other people, so that the whole way the economic system worked encouraged selfishness and competitiveness. Under capitalism you had to be selfish to survive, because the whole society was based on exploitation and competition. But once that was changed and you had an economic system based on planning and co-operation for mutual benefit, people would no longer *need* to be selfish and competitive in their outlook. Moreover all the thousand-and-one social pressures which affect people's values and ambitions would operate in a different way. To do a 'smart deal' or find some new way of getting something for nothing (in reality, at someone's else expense) would no longer be considered clever, but, instead, contemptible.

Under communism the possibilities that opened up for mankind were, Marx held, literally limitless. Nothing would hold back scientific progress, and through new technological developments (like automation, for example) work could become all the time easier and shorter. As a result, an enormous increase in leisure-time would be possible and people would be able to use this not just to relax and overcome their tiredness, but to develop entirely new interests and skills. Why should not a man have two professions, and the electrician decide, in his thirties, to become a journalist? And would he not, as a result, be a much better journalist for having been a practising electrician? Was this not the way to break down the over-specialization which had become one of the limiting aspects of modern society? Under communism, Marx was confident, the age-long separation between mental and manual work would be broken down: the cook and the philosopher would no longer live in different worlds. He looked forward to the development of the 'all-round man' who could be sane and well-balanced because he did not have to spend his life specializing on some tiny aspect of production.

All this is summed up in the thought expressed by Marx and Engels in *The Communist Manifesto*:

'In the place of the old bourgeois society, with its classes and class antagonisms, we shall have an association in which the free development of each is the condition for the free development of all.'

In other words, the founders of Marxism believed that once class division and economic exploitation have been abolished, men will become, to a degree almost inconceivable to those who live out their lives in class society, free to develop their own individual peculiarities and possibilities. And this will be so because the old opposition between the individual and society will have been removed. The individual will no longer think of himself as being in conflict with society or prevented by society from realizing his ambitions. On the contrary he will see society quite differently as something without which he himself could not live and grow and whose every advance in joy and knowledge includes and involves him too. For society, in the view of Marxism, has no meaning save as a collection of individuals, and the individual has no full existence save as a member of society.

The transition to communism involved, Marx believed, the changing of human nature. This did not deter him, for he thought that human nature, like everything else, was always changing and being changed. He saw the business of changing human nature as the greatest and most exciting challenge men have to face. But that is something we must leave till the next chapter.

CHAPTER 4

MARX'S PHILOSOPHY

KARL MARX developed his philosophy in the course of his work and struggles. What we call his philosophy is the body of general principles which, as he himself recognized, lie behind his various activities—as economist, as historian, as revolutionary, and as ordinary human being, husband and father—and draw them together into a consistent whole. A philosophy is a system of thought, a world-outlook, what emerges when a man draws all his various thoughts about different subjects together and gets them into order.

A man's philosophy is not something he keeps in a special little box, or even book, marked 'Philosophy'. Or, if he does, that is not the kind of philosophy Karl Marx was interested in. A good deal of Marx's philosophy will have emerged already from the other chapters of this book. And that is how, Marx himself believed, such things work. A man does not start with a clear, complete, logical system of thought, all worked out to the last comma, and then solemnly live his life according to his philosophical principles. His system of thought arises out of his life, out of his home background, his education, his work, and the way he grapples with the problems he has to face.

That is why we did not begin, in this book, with an outline of Marx's philosophy, and then try to apply it to his various activities. For that might have given the impression that he began with a set of cut-and-dried ideas, some sort of dogma, and then tried to impose it on the world around him. And this is precisely what Marx tried not to do.

Marx was a materialist. It is necessary to understand exactly what this word means, for it is often misunderstood. In everyday talk, in the newspapers and sometimes in the writing of people who ought to know better, the word 'materialism' is used to mean being concerned only with material things—food, comfort, and above all, money. The 'materialist', in this everyday loose usage, is the man who cares only for money and material possessions, as opposed to decent values—kindness, unselfishness, honesty. When you hear our present civilization being attacked for its 'materialism' what is nearly always meant is that people are, in the speaker's view, interested only in buying and selling, getting rich quick, rather than in living according to high principles and good moral values.

Now it is clear that Karl Marx, in this commonly used, loose sense of the word, was not a materialist at all, either in his life or in his ideas. He was a man who cared nothing for money or social success or material belongings; and he had nothing but contempt for this kind of materialism. Yet Marx called himself, in the philosophic sense of the word, a materialist and regarded philosophic materialism as the basis of his ideas.

What is meant by materialism in this particular philosophical sense? It is the philosophy which says that the world really exists, that it is *there* quite independent of us or our thoughts, and that our ideas, true or false, are reflections or distortions of an actual material reality, and arise not out of the blue but out of attempts to understand and solve actual problems.

Thinkers who are not materialists assume that ideas or moral principles are simply there and have an existence and validity independent of the world and its development. 'In the beginning was the idea' is a good example of non-materialist thinking. The materialist says you cannot begin with an idea, for every idea is an idea about something. Therefore the very existence of an idea assumes the existence already of something else. That something else is material reality, some aspect of the physical universe. The materialist says that the question 'who or what created the physical universe?' is a meaningless question. The universe is there and always has been and always will be. It was never created. And if you object 'That is very hard to imagine or grasp', the materialist replies, 'Yes, indeed, it is hard to imagine or grasp for it is outside human experience. But the alternative possibility—that the universe was at some time *not* there—is impossible to grasp.'

You can look at the question in another way. We have said that to the materialist the very existence of an idea assumes the existence of something else—what it is an idea *of* or *about*. It also, to the materialist, assumes the existence of something to think *with*. You cannot think, he says, without a brain. There was no thought until there were creatures with brains. When your brain stops functioning, you cease to think.

Engels and Eleanor Marx on the platform at the May Day Parade in Hyde Park, 1891

A demonstration organized by the International Working-Men's Association, London, 1871

If your brain is damaged, you cannot think straight. That very phrase 'to think straight' is significant. It means that unless thoughts correspond with something else—the way the universe works—we reject them as mere nonsense, a distortion of some kind. When we say something is true we mean that it is in accordance with the facts, with objective reality. This is the kind of argument that leads the materialist to the conclusion that material reality is what everything starts from.

The principal objection to the materialist approach to philosophy before the time of Marx was always that it could not explain the phenomenon of change, which means the introduction of new elements into a situation. If thoughts are simply reflections of an outside reality, if human beings are entirely the product of what is already there—environment, hereditary factors, past experiences and so on—then it is not easy to see how the element of change or progress is introduced.

This was, Marx believed, the great weakness of previous materialist philosophies. They tried to explain life in a mechanical way, and this was unsatisfactory for two reasons: in the first place, it failed to give a true enough account of the way things actually happened; and in the second, it tended to make people feel themselves to be at the mercy of forces over which they could have no control whatever.

Marx and Engels, therefore, introduced a new element into materialist philosophy which they believed corresponded to the way things actually worked. They called themselves materialists, to indicate that they believed that material reality was absolutely fundamental, but they added the word 'dialectical'. The Marxist philosophy is called 'dialectical materialism'.*

Without going into details of a complicated subject, we can say that the new element which Marx brought to materialist philosophy was a realization of the continuous changingness and inter-connection of things. Marx himself said that he owed this realization to the German philosopher Hegel, who had taught at Berlin University.

Materialists before Marx had tended to see matter itself as something static, something simply there, a lump or, at best, an enormous number of extremely small lumps. But Marx and Engels said that such a view of matter was unscientific. Matter itself, they pointed out, is in a state of continuous change. Sometimes the change is so slow as to seem non-existent; but this is an illusion. Everything changes. New forms of matter appear. There *is*, in this sense, creation. But the creative process is indeed a process, arising out of the very nature of matter itself.

The most common everyday misunderstanding of materialism as a philosophy is that it makes the material factors of existence—food, clothes, and so on—the only

* *Dialectical* was originally used by the ancient Greeks to describe a way of arriving at the truth by means of argument between opposing points of view (e.g. Plato's *Dialogues*). Later philosophers (especially Hegel, who influenced Marx so much) used the word because they wanted to express the view that life itself developed as a result of the clash of conflicting forces. Whereas non-dialectical thinking tends to see reality as composed of unchanging, absolute, eternal features, dialectical thinking sees conflict and struggle as the very essence of life's processes.

one and ignores spiritual values. This misunderstanding arises as a rule because people associate the philosophy of materialism with the loose unphilosophical use of the word already mentioned. They assume that because Marx held that material things are fundamental, he thought them in every sense more important than non-material things. But this is not so. Marx knew quite well that man does not live by bread alone. He did not think that to have a lot of money was more important than to live a good life. What he did, as a materialist, believe is that without bread you cannot live any sort of life at all, good or bad.

Engels, in his speech at Marx's graveside, put the materialist position very clearly. He said:

'Mankind must first of all eat, drink, have shelter and clothing, before it can pursue politics, science, art, religion, etc.; therefore the production of the immediate material means of subsistence . . . forms the foundation upon which the state institutions, the legal conceptions, the ideas on art, and even on religion of the people concerned have been evolved, and in the light of which they must, therefore, be explained.'

In all societies, without exception, men associate in order to produce their material means of subsistence without which they cannot live. Social production is therefore 'primary' in the precise sense that social life begins with it. Marx maintained, therefore, that in this very simple sense the higher spiritual values are dependent on the material ones, and that you can never in fact completely separate spiritual values from their material basis. Kindness is a spiritual value: but you cannot be kind in a vacuum. To be kind means to help other people; but you cannot help a man who is starving except by giving him something to eat. No amount of kind thoughts or feelings will do instead. In fact, to be able to be kind in such a situation means to be in a position to put your kind feelings into practice, to act as well as to feel and think. And actions take place not in the mind, but in the material world.

This brings us to the other important emphasis in Marx's philosophy, what he called 'the unity of theory and practice'. This means that the test of a theory or idea is whether it corresponds to the facts, not whether it sounds good. It is the same with people. You cannot judge a man simply by what he says or thinks: what is really important is what he does. If his actions, his practice, are outstandingly good then you begin to feel that there is probably something of value in the theories behind them. But we do not admire a man with high-sounding ideas who never puts them into practice. To use a very homely phrase which exactly catches Marx's meaning: 'The proof of the pudding is in the eating.'

You can see how the two points link up—the emphasis that material reality is the basic reality and the emphasis that ideas have to be tested in action. Lenin, the greatest of later Marxists, always referred to Marx's philosophy as 'a guide to action'.

You can also begin to see the significance of that famous

sentence of Marx's which is inscribed on his gravestone: 'The philosophers have only interpreted the world in various ways: the point, however, is to change it.' This sentence is often misunderstood. People who have not thought about it sufficiently assume Marx meant that philosophy is a waste of time, for heaven's sake let's stop thinking and get into action; it is more important to change the world through revolution than to bother about philosophy.

But Marx's meaning was deeper than this. If he had not had the greatest respect for philosophy he would not have written books about it. He did not believe in change just for the sake of change, action for the sake of action. He was not one of those cynics who think that what is right is what you can get away with, and that to stick to one's principles at difficult moments is simply daft. What Marx was saying in that sentence is that the weakness of previous philosophers had been that they had not analysed correctly the relation between man and the universe.

Either, Marx argued, the philosophers had looked on men as more passive and less free than they actually are, and seen them as creatures completely at the mercy of outside forces; or else they had made the opposite mistake and imagined men to be more free than they actually are. Either mistake Marx thought to be disastrous. For if you see man as merely passive, merely a product of the situation he finds himself in, then you are bound to under-estimate his ability to influence and change things. While if you see him as absolutely free, an independent non-material being who simply happens to be spending seventy years or so on this planet, then you fail to see him as he is and totally misunderstand the *way* he can influence and change things. We will return to this question in a moment.

Marx saw the individual as born into a particular situation and therefore—at the outset—formed by that situation. But he also saw the individual as having an *active* relationship to the world into which he is born. You are basically the product of your surroundings: if you had been born at a different time in a different place to different parents you would be a different person. But the way you develop, the kind of person you become, is not pre-ordained. It depends on a great many factors and influences, including yourself. It depends above all on what you *do*. Marx held that people discover the truth about things, about the outside world and about themselves, through their actions. A scientist finds out more about the world through experiment. Newton grasped his principle, and Archimedes his, not simply by thinking, but because things happened. You get to know more about yourself, Marxist philosophy says, less by introspection (thinking about yourself) than by actually setting about trying to solve your problems. Indeed, it is only when you try to solve a difficult problem that its nature becomes clearer. Man gets to understand the world through trying to cope with his problems, through *changing* things.

That is what Marx was driving at in his statement about other philosophers merely interpreting or thinking about the world. He was not saying that these philosophers would have been better men if they had been less interested in philosophy and more interested in politics. He was saying that they would have been better philosophers if they had been more interested in politics. For in that case they would have understood better the true relationship between thought and action, a relationship which applies not only to politics but to every sphere of human life.

What are some of the points that follow from these underlying principles of Marx's philosophy? It will not, obviously, be possible to discuss all sides of dialectical materialism: we can only pick out a few important ones.

Marxism as a Science

Marx always referred to his work, whether on philosophy, history, or economics, as 'scientific work', and he and Engels claimed that their approach to all problems was a scientific one. They did not claim that science has as yet the answer to every question that men ask, but they did believe that there is nothing about the universe that is unknowable. There are questions which men are as yet unable to answer and may not be able to answer for thousands of years; but this is because our knowledge and perhaps even our brains are as yet insufficiently developed. But man's knowledge and his capacity for coping with the world are constantly increasing, and Marx would set no limit on the possibilities of human development.

One of the consequences of this outlook was Marx's insistence that all subjects have to be studied with reference to their history and development. He did not believe in 'revealed' ideas, truths appearing to mankind from out of the blue, or in dogmas which could not even be questioned. Instead, he held that all ideas and theories —whether true, false, or partly true—have arisen at particular times as a result of men being faced with particular problems and therefore asking particular questions.

The primitive savage does not ask the question, 'Is it wrong to kill the prisoners you take in war?' It simply does not occur to him to ask it, for in a society in which there is no surplus production, no spare food, there is nothing to do with prisoners except to kill them: therefore it is impossible at this stage of society for a theory to arise which maintains that prisoners-of-war should be treated humanely. Similarly in modern society no one holds the theory that if you sacrifice a live goat the crops will grow better. Modern man has solved that particular problem, and such ideas will never again be current.

In other words, what Marxism implies is that there are *no* eternal truths, *no* absolute unchanging moral values. The very idea of truth changes as man's needs and knowledge change. We cannot in the nature of things know what questions people will be asking in five hundred years' time.

As society advances to higher forms, moral standards become possible and necessary which in primitive societies are quite impossible. Among the ancient Greeks, for all the splendours of their civilization, it was not a crime to own another man, a slave. Yet under socialism, Marx pointed out, it would be considered a crime even to employ another man for wages if that meant that you were making profit out of him. Moral standards change according to man's social progress.

This does not mean, though, that Marx said there was no such thing as truth or that no morality was higher than another. Quite the contrary. Tested knowledge about the world—whether the world of nature or of man—Marx held to be objectively true. It is true, for instance, that if the pressure and volume are constant, water boils at 100° C. But such scientific facts are true because they do *not* postulate an eternal state. If the pressure is different or the composition of water changes the statement that water boils at 100° C. is no longer true. Objective truths of a scientific kind never remove truth outside the realms of space and time, even though our conceptions of space and time themselves change and grow more complex.

Marx and Religion

Marx believed that religions, like other ideas and movements, arose at particular stages in the development of mankind for reasons which it is possible for the historian to explain. He also believed that the same religion tended always to change its emphases and even its dogmas as society changed. The stress on the individual and his conscience in Protestant Christianity, for instance, he thought to be due to the rise of the capitalist class with their emphasis on individual enterprise.

He did not believe any religion to be true, though he did not deny that at certain points in history certain religious movements had been progressive, and certain ideas, even though expressed in religious terms, valuable. But the very idea of a god Marx held to be unscientific. His view was not that God had created man, but that men had created gods in order to try to explain what they were unable, at that particular epoch, to understand. The only way primitive man could explain the eruption of a volcano was by associating it with the anger of a god; once men discovered what really caused an eruption they ceased to need such explanations.

One of the chief reasons for the attraction of religion to large numbers of people in the epoch of class society was, Marx believed, the unsatisfactoriness of their lives. They turned to religion for a hope, an escape from pain, which they could not find in their actual lives. This was what Marx meant when he once referred to religion as 'the opium of the people'. He did not despise people for turning to religion, but he felt sure that in a society in which they could satisfy their needs and hopes better they would cease to be religious.

Two further points are worth making in this connection. In the first place, Marx was not in favour of persecuting people for their religious ideas. Holding as he did that people would continue to believe in gods just as long as some lack in their lives led them to feel the need for such a belief, religious persecution seemed to him not only cruel but useless. You cannot kill an idea, Marxists hold; you can only change society in such a way that certain ideas become out of date and cease to correspond with people's understanding of reality.

Secondly, Marx did believe that organized religion was frequently used by the ruling class in class society for their own purposes. To encourage the belief that a man should be content with that station in life 'into which it has pleased God to call him' was, he pointed out, very useful to the privileged few who had been called into a life of leisure. He also pointed out that in most class societies the Church itself is a very considerable material power, often one of the largest landowners in the country, and that the dignitaries of the Church normally form a part of the ruling class or 'Establishment'.

Changing the World

As we have seen, Marx's philosophy emphasizes all the time the question of change. It is not simply that Marx thought that many things in his time *ought* to change or be changed: his point was that everything in fact *does* change, whether we like it or not. The important question was, therefore, that men should ensure that things changed, in so far as possible, in the right direction. Everything is all the time either growing and developing or else decaying, moving towards extinction. Nothing stands still.

This applies, Marx insisted, to man himself. He argued that human nature is itself constantly changing. It is true, of course, that modern man has many things in common with primitive man. He needs to eat; he produces children; he feels pain and fear and joy. But what he eats, the way he feels towards his children, what makes him frightened or glad—these change as society changes. The fact that we control our appetite is just as important as the fact that we have appetites. And this very ability to control himself and his environment to a degree which even the most advanced animal cannot, is one of the things that makes man human, distinguishes his nature from that of other creatures. Human nature has changed considerably during the relatively short time that there have been men on earth, Marx and Engels argued, and either human nature will continue to change or else man himself will become extinct, like the dodo or the brontosaurus.

But the question remained: *How* does man change himself? And Marx's answer is clear, though it is not perhaps easy to understand. Marx maintained that man changed himself by changing the world. It was one of the great mistakes that previous philosophers and reformers had made to imagine that man could be changed by preaching. You do not change the world, said Marx, by first trying to change people's ideas. It is the other way round. In so far as you are able to change the world you are able to change man's ideas.

Marx did not deny, of course, that individual people could be changed or 'converted' by being preached to, or that they became, as a result of such conversion, able to influence the development of things. But he held that such conversion only became an effective force if the material conditions were already favourable.

It was true, for instance, that the preaching of socialist ideas and the spreading of socialist propaganda was a necessary part of the struggle to bring about the socialist revolution. But unless the working class was beginning to learn through its own experience, through its actions and its life, what capitalism was really like, the preaching and propaganda would fall on stony ground. Before you sow the seed you must have ground to sow it on and must also have worked to prepare the ground.

Marx believed that human beings were capable of tremendous change. He would have been bitterly and sardonically opposed to the idea, for instance, that you can measure a child's intelligence once and for all at the age of eleven and that this shows whether or not he is capable of receiving serious education. Marx considered every normal human being to be capable, *given favourable conditions*, of developing his abilities to a high degree. But he did stress that the important thing was the favourable conditions. He did not say that it was impossible to be good in a bad society. But he did believe that it is only in a good society that you can reasonably hope that most people will lead good lives. And in a bad society you cannot be good unless you struggle against the bad things in that society and try to change them.

The notion of changing the world is fundamental to Marx's philosophy. And it is linked up with the idea of freedom. It is hard to understand the one without the other. Marx and Engels did not believe that anyone is ever absolutely free. According to them a man's freedom of choice is always limited, limited by the hard facts of the situation he is faced with. But this does not mean that freedom is unimportant. On the contrary, it means that man becomes free to the extent that he is able to master and control the world.

Science was therefore seen by Marx and Engels as supremely important in man's struggles to be more free. For in so far as, through science, man comes to understand the outside world, he becomes master of that world and is free to use and extend his powers. And in so far as he masters the science of society, he can get control of social and human problems and is free to solve them.

Some philosophers see the ideas of power or control as being the opposite of the idea of freedom. But to Marxists, man's freedom increases with his power. You cannot be free in any situtation unless you are in control of that situation. Or, as Engels put it, 'Freedom lies in the recognition of necessity'.

It is important to give full weight to this side of Marx's teaching, for otherwise it is impossible to understand why Marxist ideas have captured the imagination of millions of people and inspired them to live and work and sacrifice. Marx did not stress in his thinking only the things which are unsatisfactory in the world as it is. He held out the possibility of a far better world in which people would be able, he felt sure, not only to be better-off in the material sense, but to live better and more worthwhile lives.

Marx's is an optimistic philosophy because he saw

men and women as free to take the world in their hands and shape it according to their needs and dreams. He did not think that this was something easy; he saw human life as involving tremendous battles for the overcoming of difficulties and ignorance, errors and false ideas. He was well aware of the weaknesses of human beings as well as their strengths. But he emphasized the strengths. He saw the world as a changing world, and men and women as capable, in changing it, of rising to new heights and glories.

PART THREE

DO MARX'S IDEAS MATTER TODAY?

IF THE work and ideas of Karl Marx did not matter today, I would not be writing this little book and you would not be reading it. We should not consider either of these activities worthwhile. Let us assume, then, that Marx's ideas have had a good deal of influence, and try to assess it.

Three particular questions arise: How far have Marx's theories been proved true by later events? How much influence have his ideas had on later thinkers? How far have his ideas changed the world since his time?

This chapter will be an attempt to answer these three questions. It will not be an attempt to say whether or not Marxism, as a system of ideas, is true. That is for you to decide.

How far have Marx's theories been proved true by later events?

Marx, as we have seen, considered himself a scientist. That is to say, he believed his approach to social and historical questions was as scientific as, say, Darwin's approach to biological questions. Engels underlined this point when he said, 'Just as Darwin discovered the law of evolution in organic nature, so Marx discovered the law of evolution in human history'.

Now one of the features of scientific laws is that they

give men the ability to predict the way in which, given certain circumstances, things will happen. And, naturally, if things very clearly do not happen in the way the appropriate scientific law leads us to expect, then we conclude that there is something wrong with the law and that it must at least be modified. So it is fair to ask the question about Marx's own ideas: Have they stood the test of time, or are they out of date? Did he foresee what the 20th-century world would be like?

Marx did not look on his writings as a new kind of Bible; nor did he regard his conclusions as unchanging or unchangeable dogma. 'Doubt everything' was one of his favourite mottoes. He knew quite well that the 20th-century world would be very different, in plenty of ways which he could not possibly foresee, from the world he lived in himself. And though he thought that a scientific approach to social and political questions could indeed reveal the tendencies at work within a particular society and make it possible to foresee in general terms where those tendencies would lead, he made no claim to be able to give detailed prophecies about the future.

Marx anticipated that, as time went on, the capitalist system would decay and a socialist system arise. The general development of human society which he foresaw was that capitalism as a system would be unable to solve its problems and that it would in time be replaced by world-wide communism. He thought that capitalism as a whole would get weaker and be faced with crises of increasing seriousness, economic and political. He would undoubtedly have regarded such things as the First and

Second World Wars, the periodic economic crises of the 20th century, and the break-up of the colonial empires of the Western powers, as confirmation of his general view of the way capitalism was going. And there is little doubt that he would have seen the Russian Revolution of 1917 as the first decisive step in the coming of communism. The first words of *The Communist Manifesto*, written in 1848, are 'A spectre is haunting Europe: the spectre of communism'. The fact that these, or words like them, could and have been written so often in our own time would have been seen by Marx as a striking confirmation of the general truth of his social theories. But of course only time will tell whether in fact communism will replace capitalism in the world as a whole.

Marxists do not think that Marxist thought ended with the deaths of Karl Marx and Frederick Engels, any more than the study of evolution ended with the death of Darwin. Later socialist thinkers, especially Lenin, have used Marx's methods of approach to analyse the later developments of the capitalist system. It was Lenin who, on the basis of what had been happening in the world in the thirty years after Marx's death, put forward the theory of 'Imperialism' as the final, 'highest' stage of capitalism.

Marx himself had noticed how, as capitalism developed, there was a general tendency for the big capitalists to 'eat up' the smaller firms and for economic power to pass more and more into the hands of these 'monopolies'. He had also, in his later years, taken particular interest in the growing unrest in colonial countries (i.e. countries dominated by foreign capitalists), especially India and

Ireland. It remained for Lenin to show how the growth of monopoly in the capitalist countries of the West and the more ruthless exploitation of the 'backward' colonial areas of the world which began about 1880, marked a new stage in the development of capitalism, the stage he called 'Imperialism'. In this stage of social development the entire world was to be divided up, for purposes of exploitation, by the capitalists of the 'advanced' countries in their desperate need to keep up their profits.

Two of the principal results of this development were particularly important. One was that, so long as they were able to increase their profits, the capitalists of the Western 'imperialist' countries were able to keep their 'own' working classes (i.e. the British, or French, or American) in relatively privileged conditions which in many respects blunted their revolutionary feelings. The other was that the workers in the 'backward' colonial countries of Africa, Asia, and South America would come more and more into the front line of the class struggle.

Twentieth-century Marxists claim that nothing that has happened in the last hundred years contradicts the general laws of social development which Marx discovered. But they point out that one must not expect Marxism, any more than any other scientific theory of human behaviour, to provide ready-made answers of a cut-and-dried sort. When he looks out at the world of today the question the present-day Marxist asks himself is not, 'Is the class struggle in the 20th century exactly the same as the class struggle Marx described in the 19th century?', but 'Is there, in the 20th century, still a class struggle?' For he would not expect, as a Marxist, that anything would be just the same as it was a hundred years ago. What he does, therefore, is to set about analysing the 20th-century world by using Marx's *methods*, not his conclusions. Are there still in modern Britain, he will ask, classes with interests which bring them inevitably into conflict with one another? Are workers still exploited—that is to say, do they still, by selling their labour-power for wages, enable capitalists to make a profit? Do the conflicts which nowadays arise in international politics have a class basis?

Modern Marxists believe that there is still a class struggle, though its forms are different from those of a hundred years ago, and that without the light which Marx's method of analysis sheds, it is impossible to understand at all clearly what is going on in the contemporary world. This does not mean that they think Marx was never wrong. For instance, Marx himself thought in his earlier days that the first socialist revolution would be most likely to take place in Germany. Later it was France that he had most hopes of. And though in his later years he was well aware of the significance of the revolutionary movement in Russia, it would be absurd to pretend that he had some kind of pre-vision of the occurrence or course of the revolution that took place in Russia in 1917. There can be no doubt that Marx expected the socialist revolution to begin in one of the 'advanced' capitalist countries of the West, rather than in a 'backward' unindustrialized country like Russia or China.

Does this prove that Marx's approach was faulty and his theories out of date? A number of critics of the

Marxist position have thought so, but the great majority of Marxists disagree. They hold that the contribution of later Marxists like Lenin to Marxist theory has been quite in line with Marx's own principles. They would not, as we have seen, deny that Marx was mistaken in some of his particular judgments; but they maintain that, by and large, no one in the 19th century understood as well as Marx the way the world was going, nor played so decisive a part in shaping the history of the 20th century.

How much influence have Marx's ideas had on later thinkers?

In the development of knowledge in the 20th-century world, particularly in the sphere of the social sciences (history, anthropology, economics, sociology, political theory) there can be no question that the influence of the ideas and especially the method of approach of Marx and Engels has been very great indeed.

This kind of influence is always hard to measure. For one thing, Marx himself would not have claimed to have originated all the ideas associated with his name, so that it is not always easy to say definitely, 'That is a Marxist idea; that is not'. For another, people's minds are affected even more by the general, unconscious climate of thought they grow up in than by specific single books or philosophers. Many scholars and scientists who would certainly not call themselves Marxists now take for granted certain of the ideas—such as the fact that there is a significant relationship between the development of a nation's culture and its social development—which Marx had to fight hard to establish. It is therefore not always possible to separate out completely the Marxist and non-Marxist components of a modern man's thought.

Very few Western historians today would deny that, before the time of Marx, economic history had been seriously neglected and that Marx played the major part in altering this state of affairs. As a well-known modern Oxford historian, Mr A. L. Rowse, who is certainly not himself a Marxist, has put it in his book *The Use of History*, 'One can go so far as to say that to be a good historian in our time one needs to have been something of a Marxist'. Again, most philosophers today would agree that Marxism has helped to get rid of many old and false ideas which held back the progress of earlier philosophy.

But one must distinguish between the general, rather vague sense in which certain of the ideas which we can connect with Marx have, sometimes in a rather misleading form, come to have a wide currency, and the way in which Marxism itself, as a definite system of thought, has won adherents among scholars and thinkers.

From the first Marx's ideas, though largely ignored by the 'Establishment' of the day, won some enthusiastic converts in Britain and elsewhere. One of the most notable of these was William Morris, the artist and poet, who came to call himself a communist. As to the number of 20th-century intellectuals who have committed themselves to a Marxist position, it is very great indeed. Ignoring for the moment eminent figures who have grown up in the countries where there are communist governments, one has only to mention scientists like

Frédéric Joliot-Curie and J. D. Bernal, or great figures in the cultural world like Paul Robeson and Pablo Picasso. Some of the finest writers of the century have been Marxists and proud of it: the Russian Maxim Gorky, the German Bertolt Brecht, the Irishman Sean O'Casey, the Frenchmen Louis Aragon and Paul Elouard, the American Theodore Dreiser, the Chilean Pablo Neruda, the Dane Martin Andersen Naxo; while other intellectuals, less fully committed, have made no secret of their sympathy with the communist cause in general and with many aspects of Marx's thought. Among such figures one might mention Anatole France, Bernard Shaw, Charlie Chaplin, Beatrice Webb, Jean-Paul Sartre, and Dr Hewlett Johnson, the Dean of Canterbury.

An interesting point about the influence of Marxism in the non-socialist countries of the world is that it has varied considerably according to the changing political and social situation. During the nineteen-thirties, for instance, the period of the great depression when there was serious economic crisis and unemployment in the capitalist countries and a fairly obvious drift towards a new world war, the interest in Marxism among the intellectuals of such countries as Britain, France, and America was considerable. It became quite fashionable to be a Marxist: and this tendency increased during the Second World War, when Russia and the Western powers fought side by side against Hitler's Germany, and the communists played a leading part in the Resistance movements within the countries occupied by the Germans.

Then in the post-war period of the 'cold war', when

political relations between Russia and the West became
bad and there was, compared with the 'thirties, a greater
prosperity in some of the capitalist countries, Marxism
ceased to be fashionable in the West and nearly all the
books and articles and radio talks on the subject became
extremely hostile. It ceased to be even respectable to be
a Marxist, and many of those who had previously taken
a sympathetic view of Marx's ideas decided that they had
either misunderstood them in the first place or that
those ideas had become out of date and no longer applied
to the world of the mid-twentieth century.

Such variation in the fortunes of his ideas would not
have surprised Karl Marx, but would have tended to
confirm him in his belief that the popularity of an idea
is not due simply to whether it is true or false but to the
general social situation at any given time and, in particular, to the ability of the ruling class to put across
those ideas which are most helpful to itself and its
interests. For during the same period that Marxist
ideas were becoming decidedly unpopular in the West,
and despite the revelation by the Russian communists
themselves of some extremely bad aspects in the development of the socialist part of the world, the general
influence of and respect for Marxism undoubtedly
increased enormously in the world as a whole.

This has been true not only of the countries where
there are communist governments and where Marxism
is the accepted basis of education, but also of the countries
of Asia, Africa, and South America which have recently
won independence or are trying to do so. In these parts

of the world a large proportion of the intellectuals—students and professors, scientists and artists—are turning to Marxist ideas with enthusiasm and excitement. This is, no doubt, partly because the Marxist analysis and theory of imperialism (see page 103) seems to them to correspond with their own experiences and problems, and partly because the success of the Soviet Union in transforming a 'backward' and largely illiterate country in to an advanced industrial power, with remarkable scientific and educational achievements, impresses and inspires them. The outlook behind such a transformation must—many a young African or Indian or Arab or Brazilian is bound to feel—have something of value to give to them.

How far have Marx's ideas changed the world?

When we consider the influence of Karl Marx on the modern world we all think primarily about practical rather than theoretical matters. Marx was the founder of the communist movement, and it is through the progress of that movement that we chiefly measure the influence of his ideas. When we speak, therefore, of the influence of Marxism—whether we regard it sympathetically or with hostility—we are less likely to be thinking of a row of books on a shelf than of what the communists of the world have done and are actually doing.

Since the time of Marx, new political movements have arisen all over the world which have based themselves either fully or to a considerable extent on his teachings. The object of all these movements has been, with varying emphases according to the particular time and place, to carry through a fundamental social change which aims to replace the existing state of society by a socialist society. The most powerful and challenging of all the claims of mid-twentieth century communists is a simple one: they claim that wherever in the world socialism has been established it has been established through the leadership of a Marxist political party, and that other political parties, even when they call themselves socialist, have not succeeded in carrying out a socialist revolution.

Twentieth-century Marxists do not say that everything that has happened in those countries which have had a socialist revolution is perfect. The idea of the 'workers' paradise' is not a Marxist conception. They admit that in socialist countries like the Soviet Union bad things have happened which no one, least of all a Marxist, can excuse; but they maintain that the bad things have to be seen in proportion and that they are very decisively outweighed by the good ones.

The very fact that everyone today recognizes that there is a division of the world into two different social systems, which we associate loosely with the 'East' and 'West', is itself evidence of the way in which Karl Marx's ideas have changed the world. But of course a Marxist would add that the real struggle that is going on in the 20th century is not a struggle between East and West as geographical units or even as competing 'power-blocs', but that it is, at bottom, even though non-Marxists may deny it, a class struggle. And this class struggle, he says, divides the capitalist world itself. Within the 'Western' societies, the Marxist maintains, powerful working-class or Labour movements operate which are themselves trying to carry through a socialist revolution in their particular country. The idea expressed so powerfully by Marx in *The Communist Manifesto* that the working classes of the world have an overwhelming common interest, this idea has become indeed a political force.

We must avoid the mistake, therefore, of thinking of Marxism or communism simply in terms of that huge area of the world where there are communist governments. In the Labour movement of a country like Britain, Marxist ideas have long been powerful and remain so today. The long struggle between 'Right' and 'Left' within the British Labour Party can be seen—as far as ideas are concerned—as a struggle between those (the 'Right') who reject the whole conception of class struggle and others (the 'Left') who accept a view of society and social advance influenced in varying degrees by Marxist thinking. The opening sentences of *The British Road to Socialism*, the programme of the Communist Party of Great Britain and a good example of contemporary Marxist political thinking, run:

'The Communist Party's aim is socialism, because socialism is the only way to solve the problems of the British people and end the class divisions in society.

'This has been the goal of the pioneers of the Labour movement since its earliest days. In the trade unions and Co-operative organizations, in the Labour Party and in the Communist Party, generations of working people have fought for better conditions. Many important advances have been won. But we have not yet made the decisive step forward from a capitalist to a socialist order of society. . . .'

It is necessary, if we are to make an unprejudiced estimate of the influence of Marx's ideas on the world since his time, to remember that such an influence does not always work in simple ways, for the world that Marx analysed is itself a world of great complexity.

'Communists throughout the world are united by the great doctrine of Marxism-Leninism and by the joint struggle for its realization.' So runs a sentence in the statement made in Moscow in 1960 by the representatives of the communist parties of more than eighty different countries. Communists everywhere see themselves as carrying forward the ideas of Karl Marx.

To say this, however, is to say something that may easily be misleading. For the relation of communism to Marx is not the same as, say, the relation of Islam to the Prophet Mohammed. Communism is sometimes referred to as a religion, but this is not an accurate statement. For one thing, religions always involve a supernatural element, and this Marxism denies. For another, communists, because they are Marxists, do not believe the world is changed by preaching, and they see ideas—even Marxist ideas—as in the end less important than the material reality which lies behind them.

When the communists in Moscow in 1960 talked about 'the struggle for the realization of Marxism-Leninism', then, they did not have in mind some kind of religious crusade which would fight to impose the only 'true' or 'correct' philosophy upon the world. For Marxism, as we have seen, is not that kind of philosophy.

What exactly do communists mean when they talk about the realization of Marxism-Leninism? Why do they attach such importance to Marx's ideas in their practical activities and public statements? Why, in the autumn of the year 1961, was a great new monument to Karl Marx unveiled in Moscow?

Twentieth-century communists believe that without the work of Karl Marx they could not have achieved what has been achieved in Russia, China, Cuba, and the other countries where a socialist revolution has taken place. They believe, moreover, that the ideas of Marxism will, within a relatively short time, become the dominating ideas in a socialist world. Let us try to summarize why— rightly or wrongly—communists believe this.

First and foremost, communists believe the ideas of Marxism have spread and will spread throughout the world because Marx's analysis of the world is true. Most communists are not, of course, so simple as to imagine that what is true automatically and immediately defeats what is false, that the goodies will win against the baddies just because they are good; but they hold that true ideas (i.e. ideas which correspond to the facts) have one great advantage over false ideas—that they stand the test of time. Communists are confident that more and more people in the world, like Fidel Castro in Cuba, will become Marxists as they come to see that what Marxism says corresponds with their experience. It is on this that they pin their faith, or, to use a more Marxist phrase, their reasoned confidence.

Secondly, communists believe that the ideas of Marxism, just because they are true, are profoundly helpful to human beings. If you want to solve your problems, to make life better, you have first—they say—to get a truer picture of what things are like at the moment, and then you can begin seriously to set about changing them. Communists hold that Marxism gives not merely a true analysis of what exists, but also shows what could exist, what is possible. It also, incidentally, shows what is not possible, and this can often be just as helpful as the other thing.

Marxism, its adherents believe, is helpful because (a) it shows what can be done to make life better, and (b) it gives men and women confidence in their ability to do those things. The chief reason, they say, why people put up with so much that is bad and cruel and cheap and wasteful, is that they do not see how things could possibly be otherwise than they are. Men lack self-confidence, and therefore their sights are low. Marxist ideas can help them to raise their sights, to want a world which at present they dare not want.

Thirdly, communists believe that more and more human beings will come to understand and welcome Marxist ideas precisely because they are *humanist* ideas, ideas which can serve human beings and in doing so exalt them. The touchstone of humanist values, Marxists assert, is what serves humanity. Only what serves humanity is good. The 20th-century world, they believe, cries out for ideas which unite humanity instead of dividing it. And Marxism, they say, can and will bring together people of all nations, all colours, all faiths. The last line of the communist song *The International* runs: 'The International unites the human race.' Other philosophies have preached peace and wished for peace; the Marxist philosophy, which shows men how they can achieve a united, socialist world, makes the ending of war for the first time a practical possibility. Can it be doubted, the communist asks, that humane people, as they come to understand this, will recognize the value of Marxism?

Finally, communists say that Marxism gives them help and confidence because it is a *scientific* method of approach to all the world's problems. By its very nature, therefore, it is not just a dogma—a set of conclusions—but a tool. Without such a tool, progress, they argue, is impossible. Humanity may be able to solve particular problems by luck or on the basis of trial and error. But it can make real consistent progress only when it discovers the underlying laws by which reality operates.

Marxists, then, see their philosophy as a supremely practical one. It helps men and women to change the world not only by giving them in a general way hope and confidence and inspiration, but also something much more down-to-earth—a scientifically based respect for day-to-day strategy and tactics.

This last point is one which communists put a lot of emphasis on. What is the good, they say, of wanting socialism if you don't understand how to get it? It is just as important to *do* the right thing as to *want* the right thing. Men change the world through political action; political action involves political tactics. Sometimes these are not particularly exciting, and may even seem boring or unpleasant. But, as Karl Marx showed in his life as well as in his writings, you cannot avoid the day-to-day decisions and ups-and-downs of practical politics. You cannot avoid retreats, and even defeats, if you are serious in fighting a campaign. Marxists do not expect the going to be always easy. But they believe they are fighting the most worthwhile of all struggles, the struggle to make the world a better place for men and women to live in.

The impact of Marx's ideas on our world today and in the future depends on the degree of truth which those ideas, as interpreted and acted upon by contemporary Marxists, contain. If there were not *some* truth in them, it is safe to say, they would not be the talking- and fighting-point they are today—we should, indeed, never have heard of them. Communists claim that they are the truest and deepest set of ideas which human history has as yet thrown up. Without them, they say, mankind would be that much further from solving the problems which confront the modern world.

But communists also say—and this in itself is a thoroughly Marxist thought—that even if a man named Karl Marx had not landed as a refugee in England in 1849, the ideas which today we associate with Marx's name would nevertheless still have arisen, though not of course in precisely the same way or circumstances.

To recognize, however, that Karl Marx was himself a product of his time, a man of 19th-century Europe, who could not possibly have appeared upon the scene a hundred years before he did, is not to fail to recognize his personal greatness. He was, by any standards or from any point of view, a giant among men. And his friend Engels caught the essential quality of him when he said, standing beside his grave:

'. . . Marx was before all else a revolutionary. His real mission in life was to contribute in one way or another to the overthrow of capitalist society and of the state institutions which it had brought into being, to contribute to the liberation of the present-day proletariat, which *he* was the first to make conscious of its own position and its needs, of the conditions under which it could win its emancipation. Fighting was his element. And he fought with a passion, a tenacity, and a success which few could rival. . . .

'And consequently Marx was the best hated and most calumniated man of his time. Governments, both absolutist and republican, deported him from their territories. The bourgeoisie, whether conservative or extreme democrat, vied with one another in heaping slanders upon him. All this he brushed aside as though it were cobweb, ignoring it, answering only when necessity compelled him. And now he has died—beloved, revered, and mourned by millions of revolutionary fellow-workers—from the mines of Siberia to California, in all parts of Europe and America—and I make bold to say that though he may have many opponents he had hardly one personal enemy.

'His name will endure through the ages, and so also his work!'

Principal Works of
MARX AND ENGELS

INDEX

INDEX